In Richmond, Virginia, where he is pastor of the influential First Baptist Church, THEODORE F. ADAMS annually attracts thousands for his series of talks on courtship and marriage. Here, at summer conferences and at institutes, and in his earlier pastorates, he has for 25 years been active in counseling and speaking on marriage problems. This is his first published book—issued at the request of the publishers—and at the demand of the many thousands he has helped.

Making Your Marriage Succeed

Making Your Marriage Succeed

The Christian Basis
for Love and Marriage

by

THEODORE F. ADAMS

HARPER & BROTHERS PUBLISHERS

NEW YORK

Library of Congress catalog card number: 52-13215

To
Esther
Betsy, Ted and John

Contents

Contents

Foreword

For more than twenty-five years I have been preaching a series of Sermons for Homemakers each Sunday evening in January. This book has grown out of those sermons and the lessons I have learned through counseling with hundreds of couples both before and after marriage. During these years the conviction has grown that making a success of marriage depends largely on how closely a couple follow the truths and principles of the Christian faith. Marriage is a divine institution and it cannot be at its best with God left out. The church helps to develop the kind of people who can succeed in marriage, to prepare them for their wedding day, and to give them the right start in a sacred service. It also binds them together in Christian faith and fellowship, in worship and in service. Through its ministry they find guidance in life's problems, comfort in sorrow, strength for their responsibilities and hope for eternity.

Thus stated, the theme of this book is simple and direct. There is little here that is either new or novel; there is, in fact, for the sake of emphasis, some repetition of ideas throughout the book. It is written with the hope that it may enable others to find guidance and help as they seek to make a success in the great adventure of faith we call marriage and establish happy and enduring Christian homes.

The Christian gospel does have a message for every year of life from the cradle to the grave, and for every need of life from the thrilling days of growing up and falling in love to the joys and blessings of the golden years.

Because for so many years I have been collecting material for Sermons for Homemakers, it has been difficult to locate all the sources. Every effort has been made to give proper credit and any oversight will be corrected if possible in future editions.

I must express my appreciation to all who have contributed to these messages and to the many who have encouraged me to publish them. I am especially grateful to my publishers for counsel and encouragement and to Miss Eleanor Jordan for her very capable editorial assistance.

The dedication is an all too inadequate expression of gratitude and appreciation to my wife and children. Without them the book never would have been written. They and my beloved parents have taught me much and given me the wonderful privilege of living always in a house with a home inside, a blessing which I hope will come through God's help to all the readers of these words.

THEODORE F. ADAMS

Making Your
Marriage Succeed

Chapter

I

Not Too Young

ONE Sunday night after a service in which I had preached
on some of the problems and difficulties of married life,
an eight-year-old boy was riding home with his parents. During
the discussion in the car the father asked, "Son, what did you
think of the sermon?" The boy replied thoughtfully, "You
know, I don't think I'll ever get married."

What are your chances of success in marriage when so many
homes are unhappy and so many marriages fail? How can one
marry and live happily ever after? How can one grow to be
the kind of person who can marry successfully and have a
happy home? That boy probably will marry and live happily
ever after. So can nearly anyone who is willing to live as God
teaches and to profit from the experience of others.

All of the experiences of life are in one sense a preparation
for marriage and the building of a home. Children of both
sexes play together and gradually become conscious of the
differences between them. The little boy soon becomes the
defender, the soldier, the policeman, the one who guards the
little children and plays the part of the father he will some
day be in a home of his own. The little girl takes care of her
doll as though it were her own child. She is the homemaker;

she gets the meals, sets the table and plays the part that some day will become a reality in a home of her own.

Dr. Albert W. Beaven once told about his own little girl, who came sobbing to him because her doll was broken beyond repair. As she hugged it to her heart, the father took the child in his arms and tried to comfort her in her grief. Dr. Beaven said that this was but a preparation for other troubles she would face in life—like the sorrow her own father and mother had to bear a few years later as they stood outside an isolation ward watching helplessly through a window as one of their children died. How much then both mother and father needed the arms of an Eternal Father about them and the assurance of His love and concern as they faced one of the tragic hours of life.

As children grow older they go through a period of relative indifference to the other sex. Then comes the time of growing interest, when all of life takes on new glamour and new color. Youth enters into a world of comradeship and courtship. It is a time for the making of many friends and the sharing of the joys and troubles of adolescence.

As teen-agers face the pleasures and temptations of sex and love, they need to learn as do all of us, young and old, that Christ holds the answer to all the problems that life will bring. Relations with the other sex, choices in life and eventually the home of one's dreams will be either Christian or pagan. Happy are those who decide that Christ is to have his rightful place in their own lives and in every relationship of life.

Falling in love is part of a divine plan. God wants you to know life and love, marriage and home at their very best. You will do well to remember the words of Jesus, "Have you not read that he who made them in the beginning, made them male and female and said, For this cause shall a man leave father and mother and shall cleave to his wife, and they two shall be one flesh" (Matthew 19:5-6).

The teen-age years bring many conflicts between parents who say, "You are too young," and children who say, "We're not too young at all." In the years of adolescence you are not too young to be longing for comradeship and popularity. You are not too young to want to win many friends and marry one. You are not too young to dream of marriage and a home and to look forward to the day when the scripture will be fulfilled in your life and you and the one you love will live as one.

You are not too young to feel the deep and surging sex instincts and emotions that are common to all. You are not too young to sense some of the thrills and pleasures, the temptations and dangers that sex can bring. You are not too young to realize that there is something in you that makes you want the comradeship of others and makes them want you.

You are not too young to recognize that these instincts and urges are God-given, and that the expression of sex can be kept clean and holy and dedicated to the high uses your Creator intended. If cherished and respected these God-given powers can bring to you and the one you love as partners and parents the greatest joys and privileges of life. You are not too young to learn that these same urges can be abused and misused and can bring misery and lasting unhappiness to those who mistake their purpose. You are not too young to feel something of the moving power of sex and the longing and desire that draw man and woman together for the completion that only true love can give. Benjamin Franklin once said, "It is a man and woman united that make the complete human being. Separate she wants his force of body and strength of reason. He wants her softness, her sensitiveness, her acute discerning. Together they are more likely to succeed than apart."

You are not too young to love and to want to be loved, if you use that word "love" in its highest and finest sense. You are not too young to experience some of the early thrills that love can bring—the so-called "puppy love," the crushes, the beginnings of real love, the exciting days when you love one person one month and somebody else the next month. That is part of life and of the emotional development that goes on in every growing person.

You are not too young to need to learn that there are different kinds of love. Some love is impersonal, such as your love of your country or your school or your church or a cause. True love at its best is a very personal relationship, so intimate and discerning that with the eyes of love you see things in the other that no one else senses. Some personal love may be parental, childlike, or fraternal, but the deep mating love so essential to marriage has quite different qualities and is an experience that must grow. Your capacity for that type of love must grow too, and will, as you become older. A marriage often fails because the couple that married too young have not had time to develop the capacity for a lasting mate love.

Every experience of genuine friendship and comradeship contributes to the growth of true love. This is beautifully stated by Mary Carolyn Davies as she says in "This Is Friendship":

> I love you, not only for what you are, but for what I am when I am with you.
> I love you, not only for what you have made of yourself, but for what you are making of me.

I love you for the part of me that you bring out.

I love you for putting your hand into my heaped-up heart and passing over all the frivolous and weak things that you cannot help seeing there and drawing out into the light all the beautiful, radiant things that no one else has looked quite far enough to find.

I love you for ignoring the possibilities of the fool in me and for laying firm hold of the possibilities of good in me.

I love you for closing your eyes to the discords in me and for adding to the music in me by worshipful listening.

I love you because you are helping me to make of the lumber of my life, not a tavern, but a temple, and of the words of my days, not a reproach, but a song.

I love you because you have done more than any creed could have done to make me happy.

You have done it without a touch, without a word, without a sign.

You have done it by being yourself.

After all, perhaps this is what being a friend means.

In the first chapter of a century-old wedding booklet entitled *Married Life* Joseph Belcher talks about the importance of love and marriage. He says, "The deep trust with which a maiden casts her all of earth, her chance for all of heaven into one mortal hand, the confidence with which she turns her every thought to him, her more than brother and her next to God, has never yet been shadowed out in words or told in song." Love is so rich and so deep that when it really comes it takes all that you are and all of your life to express its full meaning.

Love also hallows and helps to control the sex impulse. Sex is something precious and powerful. It is not to be regarded lightly or debased or betrayed, but to be cherished as one of God's great gifts to life and love. It has three functions in life:

(1) The assurance of the reproduction of the race, for which reason God made it such a strong and instinctive urge; (2) the giving of pleasure and satisfaction to husband and wife as they share in mutual expressions of their love; (3) the unification of husband and wife as it promotes harmony between the two and binds them together as one. The New Testament says very plainly: "They two shall be one flesh" (Matthew 19:6).

Just because you are physically mature enough for sex experience and just because you may be in love does not mean that you are ready for marriage. If you are still in your teens, it is probably unwise for you to marry. Though it is perfectly true that some teen-age marriages can and do succeed, the percentage of failure is frightfully high. Nearly half of those who come to me with marriage problems and broken homes acknowledge that the difficulty is largely because they married either too young or too hastily or both.

The ideal age for marriage for a girl is from twenty to twenty-five; for a man, from about twenty-two to twenty-seven. The difference is due to the fact that girls usually mature earlier than men. You can marry sooner if you are above average in maturity and have other factors in your favor. Many, of course, marry when older and find their marriage fully successful.

Adolescents should not go steady too long with one person but should take time to cultivate many friendships. Each such relationship adds to your experience and enriches your own personality. Beware of getting too involved with any one individual under circumstances that may subject you to too great temptations to physical excess or lead to a relationship you will regret.

Often as I talk with young couples about marriage and they tell me how much they are in love, I ask, "Have you ever been in love before?" After an embarrassed pause each will admit, "Well, I thought I was in love once, but I'm really in love now." Then we can face together the fact that love is a growing experience and that, as a rule, young people fall in love, not once, but a number of times before they actually marry.

Sometimes it really is love at first sight, and you actually marry the person with whom you first fall in love. More often it happens that you marry the first person for whom you have that basic mate love that is essential to happiness and success. That person will usually be fairly close to some ideal that you have cherished consciously or unconsciously for your life partner.

It needs saying again and again that your experience of true love strengthens and adds to that experience. You usually start out with a crush on someone of the same or the opposite sex. Later you are in love with love. You may think you are in love with one person after another, though in reality it is with the delightful experience itself. These sudden infatuations come and go, though some of them are deeply moving experiences. Mere sex appeal, popularity, good looks, physical prowess, and similar traits enter into infatuation, whereas in true love you also care for a person's own worth. In infatuation the other person may be though of as one you would like to possess for your own gratification or pleasure. In real love you feel that the other is so precious that you seek his or her happiness and welfare. Infatuation is characterized by insecurity, wishful thinking, varying moods, loss of ambition and appetite, but true love brings a growing sense of security and well-being.

Infatuation may fade away quickly, but true love endures the tests and trials of life. "Now abideth faith, hope, and love, these three; and the greatest of these is love" (I Corinthians 13:13).

What, then, are some indications of the love you should seek? How can you know when you are really in love? One of the finest answers to that question comes from Dr. Newell Edson who, in *Choosing a Home Partner,* has put into words about a boy's attitude toward a girl some of the tests of true love:

> The awakening of sex attraction.
>
> A general interest in all the other says and does just because it is she.
>
> Common tastes and ideals and standards without serious clashes.
>
> A strong desire to be with her and a greater happiness when you are with her than when you are with anyone else.
>
> A feeling of unrest and dissatisfaction when you are separated.
>
> A genuine comradeship at all times and a willingness to give and take.
>
> An eagerness to consider her opinion and judgment.
>
> A feeling of pride when you compare her with anyone else.
>
> A wealth of things to say and do when you are together.
>
> She appeals to the finest that is in you and always brings out the best in you.

Christian marriage is based on the enduring love of one man and one woman for each other, a love that grows out of their own choice and desire. Such a love is both human and divine, pure, clean, and holy.

What a difference true love makes. You can see it in the

contrasting stories of Samson and Jacob. Samson was moved largely by physical desire when, seeing a woman he wanted, he simply said, "Get her for me." The end of such a relationship could only be misery and death, as it was. Jacob, on the other hand, was moved by such a genuine love that "he served seven years for Rachel, and they seemed to him but a few days so great was his love for her" (Genesis 29:20). True Christian love has power to shape and bless and change the whole course of your life.

Marriage is what two make it, two who differ physically and emotionally. They come from different families and are two different personalities. In founding a new home they start out on a great adventure of faith as they attempt to live and love and be at their best with each other. The wonder of it all is that marriage works as well as it does, not that it fails sometimes. How can you be sure that yours will be a lasting relationship? Dr. Clifford R. Adams in *Preparing for Marriage* suggests some questions you might well ask yourself before you go too far:

Do you have many common interests and things you like to do together?

Are you proud of this prospective partner, with nothing really to be ashamed of or to apologize for?

Do you have a strong desire to please him or her even if it means giving up your own preferences?

Do you have absolute faith and trust in what he says and what he does?

Does he have the qualities that you want for your children, or does she?

Do your parents and your close friends admire the one you are considering and approve of this match?

Can you disagree and still be agreeable and love and respect each other?

Do you have a good many friends in common?

Do troubles and crises when they come push you apart or pull you together?

Have you found yourself already thinking in terms of you two rather than just of yourself alone?

Do you already, at least in your own mind, have the wedding planned and the home figured out?

A young woman once showed me a picture of her husband who was in foreign service. The unique thing about the picture was the signature. Instead of signing his name at the bottom of the photograph, the young man had put some musical notes. I asked the young wife what they meant, and she replied, "My husband was sent overseas just a short time after we were married. He had this picture made and sent it to me. I was puzzled about the signature, too, and wrote to ask him what it meant. He replied, 'It comes from the song, *Because*.'" I asked, "Did you find just what it meant?" She answered, "Yes, I went through the song until I found those notes and the words to go with them. The signature really says, 'And pray His love may make our love divine.'"

Such a marriage made by two who are genuinely in love with each other, and who feel they are blessed and hallowed by God, will endure. Other marriages are doomed to failure from the start because they are not made of God. As Dr. A. Herbert Grey says, "Marriages fail because people fail, and people fail because they live without God." The Bible teaches us that "the house of the righteous shall stand" (Proverbs 12:7). Jesus stressed this in the closing verses of the Sermon on the Mount as he pictured the houses that can stand the stress of life and those that fail and fall. God does not enter into many a modern marriage. The couple may want a preacher to marry them, but too often that is about all the interest they have in the church and religion. Neither one is actively Christian. They have no active church ties, no real spiritual bond, no sense of the presence of God in life. No wonder their marriage fails. On such an insecure foundation their house tumbles in and falls when the storms of life beat upon it.

Others who enter into marriage in the right way say, "God bless our home," and mean it. They seek God's blessing in a sacred marriage service, and for that holy hour they go to the church of their choice. Both are Christians and the God before whom they bow is no stranger. They have a genuine spiritual bond that hallows their every relationship. They are bound by a common faith. They share common ideals and purposes and have found a mutual channel of service in a common church home. Good homes come to those who marry in this way and who bring to their wedding day a determination to succeed, to burn their bridges behind them, and to make the building of a Christian home their primary interest in life together. They know they do not undertake this high adventure alone. Rather, they say, "Christ is the head of this house, the unseen guest at every meal, the silent listener to every conversation." Whom God hath joined together man cannot put asunder. When the rains come and the winds blow and beat upon their house it falls not for it is founded upon a rock, the rock of a living faith.

In the play, *The Hasty Heart,* a young soldier who is a hospital patient asks his nurse to marry him. She has done much for him, and he feels a very real obligation to her. As he tells how much he is indebted to her, she wonders whether he really loves her or simply feels obligated to her. Finally she asks him, and he answers very simply, "I give you my heart because it is no good to me without you." It is out of such love and devotion that true marriage comes.

So your home, if it is to endure, must be founded upon love, and upon the rock of faith in God, rather than on the shifting sands of ignorance and fear or human sin and selfishness.

> The cornerstone in truth is laid,
> The guardian wall of honor made,
> The rock of faith is built above,
> The fire upon the hearth is love.
> Though rains descend and loud winds call
> This happy home shall never fall.

Chapter

II

So You Think You Are In Love

"HOW do you know when you are in love?" The usual answer is, "Don't worry. You'll know, all right," and as a rule that is true. You do know when it happens, and you do not need anyone to tell you, though you may need someone to guide and counsel you.

The real question, however, will be whether yours is only a passing emotional experience or whether there has come to you what someone has called, "The kind of love to marry on." Many a marriage has come to grief because there was not enough of that kind of love. Many persons who have found true happiness in marriage are eternally grateful that they did not marry the first one they thought they loved.

Courtship is one step, but only one, on the road to happiness in marriage. As you grow your ideas change, your circle of friendship widens, and your concept of love increases. The kind of man you would be happy with in your teens may not be at all the type of man you eventually want to marry. The captain of the football team may make a very striking picture when he is running for a touchdown, and your feminine heart thrills when he asks you for a date; but unless he proves that he can earn a living and provide a home, he is not the kind of man to marry. A girl may look lovely when she is dressed for some big date or special occasion; but if, as you grow in understanding, you find that she is selfish, irritable, and self-centered, she certainly is not the kind of person you want as a wife. Many are as grateful as the girl in this little verse as they look back on the people they once thought they wanted to marry:

> There was a lad when I was young
>   I worshipped in such wise.
> His name was honey on my tongue;
>   His smile, my paradise.
>
> For he was nimble-footed, bold,
>   And beautiful to see.
> But, oh, his prideful heart was cold
>   Concerning love and me.
>
> So night on night I prayed and cried
>   To win him for my dear.
> Thank heaven, God was occupied
>   With something else that year.

Courtship is important because it gives time to grow and mature, so that you will be the best person possible for the one you love, and time to help you realize the kind of person you ought to marry. As you grow, learn to pray and to seek God's guidance and help in this and other important matters.

Do you remember the scripture story of Jacob and the importance of one special night of prayer in his life? Jacob had done wrong and had to leave home. One night in a dream when far from home he realized that he was in a holy place and that God was with him. Jacob rose from that night of prayer a different and a better man because he had learned that, if he wished it, he could be sure of the guidance and presence of God anywhere and in every need of life. With that certainty of God's blessing and presence, he went on his way to seek his wife. Finally, in a distant land he fell in love with Rachel and learned how precious and how costly true love is and also that it is worth waiting for. Rachel's father would only let him have her if he worked for him seven years, but Jacob felt she was worth it all.

"If any man lack wisdom, let him ask of God and it shall be given" (James 1:5). Just as truly as Jacob needed that tryst with God on his way to find Rachel, so you and I need, and can always have, the guidance of God as we seek to build Christian homes.

If you want to make many friends and eventually win the right one, cultivate right attitudes within yourself. The Bible teaches, "In all thy ways acknowledge Him and He will direct thy paths" (Proverbs 3:6). "Whatsoever things are true, and honorable, and just, and pure, and lovely, and of good report, think on these things and the God of peace shall be with you" (Philippians 4:8). The church of your choice is a good place to meet the right kind of friends and eventually "the one and only," and also to grow to be the kind of person someone else will want to marry.

It is not enough to be in love with love. You must learn to love one person deeply, maturely, and unselfishly, so that his or her happiness is more precious to you than life itself. You should be able to say with all your heart to the one you love:

> You are my world,
> You are my sun, my star;
> There is no life for me
> Save where you are.[1]

[1] From *Bathsheba* by Virginia Rogers. Reprinted with permission of Argus Books, Inc.

As we have seen, it is important to know if your love is the kind that can issue in a successful marriage. Yours should be a complete love, embracing every realm of life with which it should be concerned, physical, emotional, mental, social, and spiritual. Let us look at a few more helpful tests:

There is and must be physical attraction, drawing you almost irresistibly to each other. True love is a deep and stirring emotional experience, providing the dynamic that will carry the two of you through all the tests and crises married life will bring.

There is a mental element in complete love, a matching of minds, characteristics and ideals, a growing understanding and a wealth of common interests and activities. The social aspect in love must also be recognized as you find increasing joy in planning your home and serving together in community and church.

One must not overlook or underestimate the spiritual element that gives love its staying power, its unselfishness, and joy even in sacrifice. Such love is born of God and those who truly love are confident that God has brought them together and shares in the whole experience with them. "If we love one another, God dwelleth in us, and His love is perfected in us" (I John 4:12).

When you think you are in love test your feeling by whether just being together makes you happy and being separated makes you restless and miserable. Do you want the other to be happy, even at the cost of your own happiness? Are you eager to help each other and do you take a genuine pride and interest in all the other says or does?

You have respect for each other's personality and ideas, a similarity in tastes, ideals, and leisure-time activities, and a genuine interest and appreciation where you differ. You have a growing understanding of each other's moods and reactions in varying life situations and a feeling of unworthiness, coupled with a determination to be worthy of such a love. You can hardly think of life without each other and are both willing and eager to change, improve, and adapt to each other. You find much to do and talk about when together, rather than a relationship and interest that is largely physical. Your whole relationship is characterized by reticence, tenderness, and humility.

True love will be revealed by such standards. So will false love or a mere infatuation which is really simply being "in love with love" instead of with a person who will become a worthy partner for life.

If you ask, "Is it possible to love two people at the same time?" then you are not yet ready for marriage. You are enjoying one of the growing periods of life, but true mate love has not yet come to you. Courtship is a time of learning how to live with other people, a time of falling in and out of love several times. Each such courtship experience helps you grow in your ability to understand the breadth and height and depth and fullness of love. Those who marry too young miss this important training. The growing friendships of the late teens and early twenties serve a very real purpose, and many couples are much more happily married because of the experiences of the years of friendship and courtship. To be sure, some people fall in love just once, and it lasts a lifetime; but most people think they are in love at least four or five times before they find the real thing.

If you think you have found true love, you can test your relationship by the following questions. If you can answer

"Yes" to all or most of them, the chances are that you are well on the way to the kind of love that is essential to lasting married happiness.

> Has he actually told you he loves you?
>
> Do you feel in your heart that he is more interested in what he can do for you than in what he can get from you?
>
> Does he spend most of his time with you to the exclusion of other girls?
>
> Has he gone out of his way to do things to prove his love?
>
> Have you gone together for at least a year?
>
> Has he maintained his love and devotion to you even when you have been separated?
>
> Does he show a real interest in the things you do?
>
> Does he defer graciously to your wishes and desires?
>
> Has he introduced you to his closest friends and does he want you with him when he is with them?
>
> Does he take pride in having you meet his family?
>
> Does he show genuine consideration and concern when you are sick or troubled?
>
> Do other people think he loves you?
>
> Does he enjoy being in your home and with your friends?
>
> Does he respect your standards in matters of sex?
>
> Does he enjoy going to church with you and is he sympathetic with your highest ideals and aspirations?

During courtship you develop your own personality through contacts with many different kinds of people. You discover in others the qualities that only time can reveal and grow yourself as you discover the qualities in your own life that are attractive to others and mean the most to them. When you find someone who really interests you, discover what each has to give to the other and determine whether you have enough in common and are alike enough to be happy together in all the varying experiences of life. This is the time to develop your common interests and discover whether you mean so much to each other that life will be complete only if you spend it together.

Self-restraint and self-discipline are also essential. Courtship can be just one physical infatuation after another, each one a little worse than the other. It is easy to fail to measure up yourself to the ideals of purity and honor that you cherish for the one you eventually hope to marry. Self-control gives way to self-seeking and self-indulgence as you explore the possibilities of pleasure in excessive and dangerous physical relationships. Love is so much more than a physical experience. It is mental and emotional and spiritual as well, a relationship that is fine and clean and holy. You say, "Well, give me some guiding tests to help me judge the temptations to sexual excesses, the petting, the kissing, and the other expressions of love that I experience."

Ask yourself the following questions, based on suggestions by Dr. Paul Popenoe, with regard to such relationships. They will help you guard against the dangers and find the real rewards of friendship and courtship.

Does it mean the same thing to both of you or is one exploiting the other just for a thrill?

Is it almost wholly physical or is it an expression of your whole personality?

Is it deceitful and furtive and shamefaced, or is it open and honest and wholehearted?

Does it increase your respect for each other?

Would you recommend your practices to your younger brother or sister?

Is it liable to lead to excesses you will regret later?

Does it crowd out other more worthwhile activities?

Is it the kind of thing of which the best crowd in your school or your church or your society approves?

Is it a satisfying fulfillment of life at its best or does it leave you dissatisfied and frustrated?

Does it deepen and enrich your friendship or does the sort of thing you are carrying on break up friendship?

Is it a wholesome preparation for your married life or may it cause attitudes in you or in others that will make happy married life difficult or give you a reputation that will make marriage impossible?

In your best moments do you feel that the things you are doing are right in the eyes of God?

Courtship is a time when you seek to mature not only physically but also spiritually, intellectually, socially, and emotionally. It takes time and effort to grow until you are a person with the ideals and faith and character someone else will want. It is important that you grow in your understanding of the true place of sex in life, so that in meeting those of the other sex you know enough about the physical and the psychological facts of life not to be misled yourself or betray someone else.

Do not heed those who would tell you that premarital sex relationships are essential to sex maturity. Far from being essential, they may actually prove to be very detrimental. They certainly are no preparation for the free and loving sex experiences of marriage. Such relationships are so furtive and so burdened with a sense of guilt in one or both as to do real hurt to mind and heart. Often they can ruin what might otherwise develop into a happy friendship or a successful marriage. In such a relationship you sin against God and yourself and the one you love. Purity and honor are a very real part of the Christian ideal as you come to maturity and prepare for marriage. God's Word puts it plainly, "Thou shalt not commit adultery" (Exodus 20:14).

You also need to grow intellectually and to develop your mind to the full as you seek to take your place in the life of your day. Set goals for yourself that will fit you for useful and rewarding employment and will make you a capable father or a worthy mother.

One of the finest Bible students and religious leaders of another generation was a man by the name of Matthew Henry. He came from a poor home and an unlettered background. As a young ministerial student Henry fell in love with a girl from a rich and cultured home. One day the father of the girl said, "I don't think you ought to have anything more to do with that young man. We don't know anything about his family or his background or where he came from." The daughter answered, "Yes, but Father, I know where he's going, and I'm going to go with him." He had proved himself worthy of her love, one to whom she felt she could trust her life forever.

Emotional growth and maturity is imperative. One of the chief causes of failure in marriage is emotional immaturity on the part of one or the other. Here are some indications or tests of genuine emotional maturity.

First of all, you should be able to carry a reasonable load of emotional tension without blowing up. All of us face annoyances and disappointments, frustrations and difficulties. The mature person faces them without going to pieces or retreating into tears of self-pity, or getting sulky or refusing to speak, or resorting to the other silly, childish ways so often seen in the immature. You certainly are not ready for a successful marriage until you have learned to face the tensions of life as a mature person.

You should have outgrown childish and foolish fears and anxieties. Little children may be afraid of the dark or afraid of falling or of loud noises. Others as they grow older are afraid of being alone. Young people are sometimes afraid of being different or of being bossed or of standing up for their own convictions. You need to grow out of such childish attitudes and beyond the years when you are concerned only about clothes and social position into the place where you can face life as an adult with a real sense of values and realities.

If you would be emotionally mature, learn to expect to be treated as a responsible partner in marriage. Some men want to be mothered and waited on all their lives instead of taking a man's place in the home as well as in society. Too often a woman expects just a delightful and continuing courtship and wants to be babied and cared for all the time, instead of getting down to the stern realities of making a home and rearing a family. Are you ready to be an equal partner in life and carry your share of the load? Are you developing the skills that will make that possible?

You should be emotionally independent of your parents and able to stand on your own feet and make your own decisions in life. You should be able to make up your own mind and bear your own responsibilities. You should be able to look frankly at your own faults and limitations and seek to correct them. You should be mature enough to get a job and hold it and to bear the responsibilities of fatherhood or motherhood.

Such growth takes time. One of the most difficult tasks of ministers and marriage counselors is to persuade people to take time, time to grow, time to fall in love intelligently and completely, time to find just the right person, and time to become the right person.

As you take time, take also the help the God who made you

for life and love is so ready and able to give. In Christ you can find the ideal person you should strive to be. Through Christ you can receive forgiveness for the sins and the failures of the past and strength to face the temptations of the future. In the faith and fellowship of the Christian church you can find the kind of person you want to marry and grow to be the person someone else will want. As you grow in other ways, be sure to grow in your understanding of what God can mean in life. Learn the power and privilege of prayer. Study God's Word and build its truth and ideals and principles into your daily life. Grow as Jesus grew "in wisdom and in stature, and in favor with God and man" (Luke 2:52). With two such lives, you and God together can build an enduring, happy, and successful home as you learn to say together:

> In hope that sends a shining ray
> Far down the future's broadening way,
> In peace that only Thou canst give,
> With Thee, O Master, let us live.

This is all summed up in a personal letter from a woman who wrote, "I've been married for five years now. God has given us one lovely child and another one is on the way. We have found in our home the heaven on earth that true love can bring. I want to share with you and perhaps through you with others the advice the preacher gave to us when he married us. He said, 'Marriage can either be heaven on earth or hell on earth. It will be as much of heaven as there is God in it, and as much of hell as there is the devil in it.' "

May God help you so to live and grow that you will have heaven in your heart and in your home.

III

Winning Friends and Marrying One

HOW can you win many friends and marry one, the right one? To answer that you must start with yourself and the kind of person you are. Do others want you as a friend? Will anyone ever want to marry you?

If you want to win many friends and eventually marry the one you love you must think not only of what you want in your life partner, but also of the kind of person he or she will want you to be. If you are really in love you will be concerned not only with what you want for yourself, but even more with what you can give to the other.

An older woman tells of thinking at one time that she was very much in love with a young man. As they were walking together one night he asked her a question, not the one she was hoping he would ask, but quite a different one. He said, "What kind of a man are you expecting to marry?" She waxed eloquent about a man who would be a combination of Clark Gable, Bing Crosby, Dwight D. Eisenhower, and John D. Rockefeller. When she finished, he did not say anything for awhile, and then very quietly asked, "And just what do you have to offer in return?"

It is important, too, that you think not only about what you want in a life partner, but also about what you need, and what you can get. Opposites do attract each other, but it takes much in common to make a success of marriage and there must be certain basic qualities and similarities if you are to be happy together.

First of all, what do you want in your life partner? Here are some qualities both should seek: Character, integrity, honesty, affection, a sense of humor, intelligence, dependability, sincerity, companionship, and consideration.

I once asked the unmarried young people in our church to list the qualities they thought essential in a life partner. The men sought the following in the woman they hoped to marry: Genuine religion, a good companion, a real homemaker, good health, character, attractive personality, neatness, cleanliness. The women sought much the same qualities, though in a different order: Character (there is no substitute for good character, for successful marriage requires such virtues as integrity, honor, and faithfulness), the ability to support a home, real religion, a good companion and homemaker, one who possesses such homely virtues as humor, patience, kindness, and above all, love.

Another group of young people listed other qualities. They felt your life mate should be a person of strong moral character, of similar Christian faith, one accustomed to attend church regularly, someone who is kind and fair, generous and considerate of others, a person with whom you share many common interests, near enough your age and educational level to assure a lifelong companionship, in sufficiently good health to make marriage desirable, willing to live within your probable income, one who loves and wants children, and one who is still a welcome companion after lengthy periods of being together.

Still another group of girls wanted primarily in their future mate honesty, love, cleanliness, a sense of humor, a good background, unselfishness, good habits, a good disposition, and domestic inclinations. Other qualities they listed were good health, a love for children, the same religion and some real religion, neatness, character, sympathy and understanding, fidelity, one you can be proud of, a similar education, and a lot of common sense.

In his book entitled *From Friendship to Marriage* Dr. Roy Burkhart writes that he asked five hundred happy and five hundred unhappy married couples what they thought were the most important qualities if the home is to succeed. Out of their experience they listed these twelve: A congenial spirit, a noncritical attitude, supreme satisfaction in making the other happy, good health, physical and emotional maturity, love of children, the same religion, similar economic background, similar social background, the ability to combat one's own moods and overlook the other's mistakes, cleanliness, and neatness.

Dr. Newell Edson gives these tests: "You should marry and you should look in courtship for a person who is closest to your ideal, a person of sterling character, one who perennially interests you in thought and speech and action; one in whom you have confidence, for confidence is the basis of faith and of love; one who wears well in all the tests of life; harmony of tastes and standards and conduct; skills of head and hand and heart; one worthy to be the father or the mother of your children; one who brings out the best in you."

To develop a real and enduring partnership you need a sense of security. Both men and women want that. You want to feel that you have a secure basis for a home, that your home rests not on a temporary infatuation or on physical desire, important though that is, but on those spiritual qualities that are the foundation of a home, faith and hope and love.

You want social approval. You want to marry someone others will like, one of whom you can be proud, someone who gets along well with other people, and who will be a real help to you in realizing your aims and ambitions in life. You want someone who can help you get ahead, who will be willing to sacrifice that your common dreams ultimately may come true.

You want a partner who is capable of genuine affection, one to whom you feel attracted physically, someone to whom you can give your love, and with whom you can share in the creation of new life. Since most lovers want children, find out how the other feels before marriage. Then, too, it may mean that if you marry a certain person you cannot have children or that there will be special risks involved in childbearing. You should face that together beforehand lest there be misunderstanding afterward.

You ought to ask yourself such questions as these:

Is this mate self-centered and self-seeking or unselfish?
Is his general mood that of being agreeable and easy to live with or is he likely to be irritable and ill-tempered and moody?
Is this person adjustable or rigid and inflexible so that you have to do all the adjusting and all the giving in?
Is this person well-balanced emotionally, able to meet the difficulties of life?
Have you known each other long enough to know how you will react to trouble in life, or do you only know each other at your best and under the most favorable circumstances?

As you grow older you will become more discerning and better able to choose the right person to share your life. Do not be discouraged if it seems to take a long time. The best things in life are worth waiting for. Above all, do not marry just to get married or become as desperate as the girl in this verse:

> At sweet 16, I first began
>> To ask the good Lord for a man;
>
> At 17, I recall,
>> I wanted someone strong and tall.
>
> The Christmas I reached 18
>> I fancied someone blond and lean.
>
> And then at 19, I was sure
>> I'd fall for someone more mature.
>
> At 20, I thought I'd find
>> Romance with someone with a mind.
>
> I retrogressed at 21
>> And found college boys most fun.
>
> My viewpoint changed at 22,
>> When "one man only" was my cue.
>
> I broke my heart at 23
>> And asked for someone kind to me.
>
> Then begged at blasé 24
>> For anyone who wouldn't bore;
>
> Now, Lord, that I am 25
>> Just send me someone who's alive!

If you know what you want in marriage and are wondering whether anyone will ever want you, take an honest look at yourself, what you are like and what you can reasonably expect to get in a mate with what you have to give. What is there about you that would make someone else want you or reject you? Are you "always a bridesmaid but never a bride"? Someone has said, "Husbands fall into three classes: prizes, surprises, and consolation prizes." Which are you likely to be?

Cultivate in your own life such qualities as these if you would be attractive to others:

Consideration	Tolerance	Optimism
Generosity	Broad-mindedness	Sense of humor
Friendliness	Unselfishness	Enthusiasm
Neatness	Naturalness	Vitality

Check yourself also for some of these things that repel other people:

Jealousy	Hot temper	Irreverence
Irritability	Air of superiority	Cynicism
Intolerance	Selfishness	Insincerity
Rudeness	Vulgarity	Lack of appreciation
Untidiness	Excitability	Discourtesy

If some of these qualities characterize you, change your ways. Be willing to admit your mistakes and apologize when you are in the wrong. Begin to develop in yourself the qualities that are most likely to attract a worthy companion. Be honest and straightforward, sympathetic and understanding with the troubles of others, and genuinely interested in all that concerns their well-being.

One marriage counselor tells of a couple who were very much in love. The girl was not as attractive and good looking as the man wished, yet he felt that on every other count they would make an ideal couple. The man soon realized that her other qualities were far more important. The girl, understanding how he felt, set about learning some of the secrets of make-up, good posture, and dressing attractively. Because of their efforts at self-improvement and adjustment, they were married and did live happily.

God's Word gives some excellent counsel in the 31st chapter of Proverbs for those who would develop an attractive personality and win a worthy life partner. As you read it through for yourself you will find a mother speaking to her son, first about himself, and then about the qualities he should seek in the woman he marries.

She says a man should have qualities of purity, faithfulness, integrity, and temperance. He should be a man who is just and righteous in his dealings with others, a man whose heart is filled with the true spirit of brotherhood for his fellow men.

Then, because she loves her son and wishes the best for him, and because she knows from experience what it takes to be a good wife, she talks far more about the girl he should seek. "A worthy woman," she says, "who can find, for her price is far above rubies. The heart of her husband trusteth in her, and she doeth him good and not evil all her days."

Carefully and thoughtfully she outlines the qualities of a woman worthy to be his wife. She must be a woman of virtue, one whom he can trust, a woman whose life is characterized by goodness, one who is fitted for her household duties, who knows how to provide the food and clothing her family will require. In the summer she will dress them in silks and satins and in the winter will be ready with their red woolens.

She is a woman with a keen business sense. She takes good care of her household budget. From her garden and other activities she provides for her family and has extra products to sell to increase the family income. She is interested in her husband's business. She strengthens and inspires him so that he is a man who is looked up to by his fellow citizens in the community. She is a woman with charming personal traits, strength and dignity, charity and kindness, a sense of humor, wisdom and industriousness. She is one who is happy and proud to be a mother. Above all she has a deep and abiding faith in God. Much of the unhappiness and misery in modern marriage would be avoided if more men and women would believe and practice these lessons from long ago.

The influence of a good home, and of someone who loves and trusts you and expects the best from you, can be a steadying influence of incalculable worth in the tests and temptations life will bring, as well as in the choice of a life partner and the building of a happy home.

On the day long ago at Gettysburg when Pickett's men were awaiting word from Longstreet to begin their fatal charge, the gallant Pickett wrote a letter to his fiancée in Richmond. When the word was finally given to move forward, he wrote in pencil on the envelope, "If old Peter's nod means death, good-bye, and God bless you, little one."

As he rode to his place a fellow officer said, "Pickett, take a drink with me. In an hour you'll be in hell or glory."

Pickett refused and said, "I promised the little girl who is waiting and praying for me down in Virginia that I would keep fresh upon my lips until we should meet again the breath of the violets she gave me when we parted. Whatever my fate, I shall try to do my duty like a man, and I hope that by that little girl's prayer I shall today reach glory."

He did achieve glory and proved worthy of the love in her heart and in his, just as many another has been strengthened and sustained by the trust and confidence of those who love him. As one young man said of his sweetheart, "I loved her in the name of God and for the ray she was of Him."

Put your life in the Master's hands. Let Him help make you what you ought to be.

A Man? What is a Man?—an earth-born soul,
Low-stooping, eye forever on the ground,
Seeking for pleasure only, or for Self,
Whose words are dirt, whose deeds are low and dark,
Who, when he works, works but to get his wage
With least and puniest effort of the soul,
Nor cares a whit for any joys of home.

Such will I never be, so help me, Christ.
A real Man make me—one upon whose shoulders
Rest heavy cares, but in whose heart are pillars
Which rest with ease,
Upon the Rock Immovable of God.
A Man who loves his home more than himself,
And brings to all therein a gift of joy
Whene'er he enters.

Such is my hope to be, such will I be.
O Christ! Who livest still to make us men,
Be Thou in me to carve and chisel well,
Chipping away the old, rough, selfish Self,
And leaving there true Man.

Such a prayer is always answered whether it be from the heart of a man or a woman. "If any man be in Christ, he is a new creature. Old things are passed away; all things are become new" (II Corinthians 5:17). When Christ has his rightful place in your life and in your home, then—and only then— will you know life and love at their best. You will win friends and marry one, and you will be worthy of the love you have won.

Chapter

IV

The Path of True Love

RECENT studies of hundreds of cases of success and failure in marriage have been made by Professors Burgess and Cottrell of the University of Chicago. In their book, *Predicting Success and Failure in Marriage,* they combine their own studies with those of others in a unique table of the factors that have been found in actual experience to contribute to success in marriage.

The length of acquaintance should ideally be two or more years.

The engagement should last six months or more.

The best age for marriage in the husband, twenty-two and over; the wife, twenty and over.

Close attachment and lack of conflict with parents.

Church attendance two to four times a month.

A similar family background.

Happiness in childhood.

Good health.

A religious marriage service.

Parents who are happily married.

Religious training at home.

Adequate sex instruction.

Many friends before marriage.

Sunday School attendance after eighteen years of age.

Just about the best assurance you can have of a happy marriage is to be fortunate enough to be born into a happy Christian home. If you were not, then you have that much of a hurdle to overcome. Many do this successfully, to be sure, but this factor is so important that you and I ought to resolve to make our homes as harmonious as possible, so happy and successful that our children will have this all-important start on a happy married life of their own.

A second important qualification is a fairly long acquaintance. It should be at least a year or better two, though it is not just a question of how long you go together, but how well you make use of the time.

The couple should be reasonably well educated and about equally matched in education, background, culture, and experience.

The age difference between a man and woman is an important consideration. The woman matures a little more rapidly than the man, and so rather naturally, a man usually chooses for his wife someone younger than himself. Yet, surprisingly enough, some of the happiest marriages are those where the woman is a little older. That perhaps is because a man often needs a little mothering along with all the other things he expects. If the couple are to have children, however, the woman should be young and strong enough for the arduous responsibilities of motherhood. Remember, too, that the right age for marriage is not determined just by the calendar. It is determined also by maturity, emotional and mental, as well as physical.

Health is precious in marriage. To be sure, there are many who marry with physical handicaps and poor health. They consider the situation in advance and make a very satisfactory and happy adjustment. If good health is yours, preserve it and protect it.

The matter of security is important. The couple should have the ability and the opportunity to earn an income sufficient to support a home on the scale on which they are willing to live. It costs more to live in the suburbs than in a rooming house down town. They have to choose the scale of life which they can afford and then make up their minds to live that way happily until they can do better. If the young man is unable to earn enough to support a family, the wife may plan to work for a time. However, if children come or sickness or hard times, the security of the marriage is imperiled if they had planned to live on two incomes. If the two come from similar economic backgrounds it makes this adjustment easier.

The possibility of military service and whether the husband in business may be transferred to another city should also be considered. The wife should be willing to go where her husband goes. If that is not true in your case, face up to it in advance.

Be sure that you have common interests in recreation and social life and a basic similarity in ambitions and ideals.

It is also important to know both families and to have their approval. When you marry you do marry the family whether you like it or not. A wise word of counsel in that regard comes from General Robert E. Lee, spoken a good many years ago. When he was a colonel, one of his officers, later to become General Hood, was thinking of marriage. At that time Lee said to him, "Let me give you a little advice. Never marry unless you can do so in a family which will enable your children to feel proud of both sides of the house."

There should be concern about the personal habits of the

one you are to marry. Drunkenness, gambling, profanity, and immorality promise little else but trouble. Beware of marrying anyone to reform him. Let him reform first or unhappiness and misery will be yours.

A wholesome attitude toward sex is essential and there should be a desire on the part of both for two or more children, if that is possible.

The two should have a vital religious faith and participate actively in the life and work of the same church. This is true for one reason if no other, that as a rule such people are easier to live with. Certainly our Christian gospel ought to produce people who are easy to live with and the kind of people God would choose to use as parents when He wants to create new lives and new personalities. Even more than that, religion provides the foundation upon which a home is to be built. Jesus in the Sermon on the Mount teaches us that an enduring home is not built upon the sands of desire or selfishness or fear or ignorance, but on the lasting foundations of faith and integrity, honesty and character, and trust in God. The Psalmist rightly says, "Except the Lord build the house they labor in vain that build it" (Psalm 127:1).

There are some things you can and should find out before marriage. You may remember the story of the little boy who wrote in a theme about Benjamin Franklin, "Benjamin Franklin was born in Boston and as soon as he was old enough to have any sense he moved to Philadelphia. He was hungry so he bought a loaf of bread and walked down the street with the loaf of bread under his arm. A young lady he passed laughed at him, so he married her and discovered electricity." After you get married you discover many things you did not know before. People who marry too young or too quickly when they are in their early teens or when they have known each other only a few days or a few weeks can hardly expect their marriage to succeed. A newspaper columnist once reported with regret that his own sixteen-year-old daughter had run away to get married. He did not hear from the girl for several days and while the parents were worried and wondering about her, the father wrote these lines called "Fledgling":

> Our little bird on untried wings
> Has vanished into the gloom,
> Leaving behind two empty hearts
> And a silent, lonely room.
>
> Into the vast and friendless world
> She fluttered on pinions frail,
> Bound for wherever small birds go
> When they take Adventure's Trail.
>
> Alas, for eager fledglings all,
> Who laugh at life's hidden reef,
> Unaware that their baby dreams
> Can easily come to grief.
>
> O God, who looks after little birds
> That fly from the mother's breast,
> Please find that lost little mite of ours
> And guide her back to the nest!

The sad thing is that so many of those fledglings do have to come back to the nest with broken hearts because their marriages were too hasty and they are too immature. You will do well to guard against that mistake both for yourself and those you love.

Differing faiths also may hinder success in marriage and even make marriage inadvisable. A recent survey was concerned with couples who differed in religion, the husband in one church, the wife in another, sometimes Protestant and Catholic, sometimes in two Protestant denominations. In such cases couples usually do one of three things. Sometimes both drop out of church. They are unable to agree on one church or the other, so they both quit, with genuine loss to themselves, their children, and the church. That happened in one fourth of the cases studied. Sometimes each continues in his own church. You can do that and have a very real bond of love and a wider religious interest, but it takes consecration and understanding on both sides to do it. You must recognize, however, that you will lose much that a common church home could bring to you and to your children. Sometimes both join the same church. If this can be done sincerely, and a common religious faith cultivated, it is the best solution. If the gap is too great, as sometimes between a Protestant and a Catholic, and it cannot be done in sincerity, it ought not to be. But it is far better than running the risk of one or both dropping out of the church in order to avoid conflict.

There is a unifying experience in a common religious faith and a church fellowship where the family can worship and serve and grow together. Face this frankly and discuss it fully before you marry, especially if you belong to widely differing faiths, both for your own sake and for the happiness of your families and your children. If parents do not make this choice for themselves, they eventually compel their children to choose, not only between churches, but also between parents, as they decide whether to go to church with father or mother.

It is much better as a rule for a Jew and a Gentile not to marry. As a very wise Jewish rabbi once said very plainly to me, "I would not advise a Gentile to marry a Jew unless that Gentile is willing to enter fully and completely into the pat-

tern of Jewish religious, cultural, family, and community life."
I had sought his counsel when a lovely Protestant girl asked
me about the wisdom of marrying a Jewish boy. She and I
talked frankly together about the differences they would face
in religion, in social life, and in family relationships, and she
very wisely decided after much thought and prayer not to
marry the Jewish boy. She is happily married now to a boy
of her faith, has a happy Christian home, and knows that
her choice was wise, though hard at the time.

Almost as difficult is the question of marriage between
Protestant and Catholic. Both groups advise against so-called
"mixed marriages" because of the division created within the
home, the high percentage of failure, the danger of the loss
of faith, and the difficult question of the church affiliation of
the children.

Many simply cannot in good conscience sign away their children to a faith they cannot accept for themselves. Here is the
kind of agreement that a Protestant must sign who wishes to
marry a Catholic according to the rules of the Catholic Church:

I, the undersigned, not a member of the Catholic Church, wishing
to contract marriage with a member of the Catholic Church propose
to do so with the understanding that the marriage bond thus con-
tracted is indissoluble except by death. I promise on my word and
honor that I will not in any way hinder or obstruct the said husband
in the exercise of his religion and that all children of either sex
born of our marriage shall be baptized and educated in the Catholic
faith and according to the teaching of the Catholic Church, even
though the said husband should be taken away by death. I further
promise that I will marry only according to the marriage rite of the
Catholic Church, that I will not either before or after the Catholic
ceremony present myself with him for marriage with a civil magis-
trate or minister of the Gospel.

There are also very real differences with reference to birth control, the number of children, and the risks of motherhood. There are difficulties with reference to worship both in the home and at church. For example, if you are a Protestant and your children are Catholic, they will be taught that they are not to participate actively in worship with you in your church.

Because of these basic differences in faith and practice, plus the reality of family pressure on both sides, it is important that you know before you fall in love just what is involved and what the basic issues really are. So often young people say, "Oh, love will find a way." If you insist on going through with such a marriage you ought to know that the path of true love does not run smoothly at all in a case like this. There are, of course, mixed marriages that are happy, but the families miss the blessing found in other homes where husband and wife and children share the same faith and worship together in the same church home.

More mixed marriages break up when the mother is Protestant and the father Catholic than when the opposite is true, because the mother has more to do with the religious life of the children. If the mother is a Catholic, she will usually abide by the vows that she and her church insisted the husband take when they married, namely, that all of the children would be reared as Catholics. If the mother is a Protestant and the father a Catholic it is very difficult for her to rear her children in a faith that is not her own, as the Catholic Church asks her to promise to do. Many a Protestant girl rebels against that after she is married. She then has her husband and his family and his church arrayed against her if she seeks to teach her children her own faith. Consequently, three times as many marriages of that kind fail.

Before you marry think well whether you want your children reared in a faith that is not your own. Think well before you let your spiritual heritage die so far as your family is concerned, especially when in a mixed marriage you are certain to have some unhappiness and you have three times as great a chance that your marriage will fail. I remember talking with one couple, she a Baptist, he a Catholic. We faced frankly what he was asking her to do, to promise to rear all her children in his faith, not hers, and to abide by the teachings and rules of his church rather than her own, with reference to the conduct of family life. I said to him, "You are asking her to do all this because she loves you. Is that correct?" He answered, "Yes." I asked, "Do you love her?" "Yes," he replied, "I do, as much as she loves me." "If that is true," I said, "would you be willing to do for her, if her church required it, what you are asking her to do for you and your church?" He answered, "I would if I could, but I can't do that. Under the laws of my church I am not free to do for her what I am asking her to do for me."

That is the case, and it is that essential element of freedom in religion that the evangelical Protestant churches are trying to preserve. That is why many feel so strongly that young men and women who are reared in an evangelical faith should cherish that faith and refuse to surrender it either for themselves or for their children, and that it is far better for them to marry someone with whom they can share a common faith and a common church home. It is easy for a young couple to say, "Oh, we'll work it out some way," but it is not that simple. The Catholic Church has very strict and rigid rules from which it will not deviate. The Protestant party in such a mixed marriage is faced with the decision as to whether to accept those regulations and abide by them and, in effect, to surrender his or her faith in so far as the next generation is concerned. Because so much is at stake it is far better to face this question and settle it for yourself and resolve to cherish your own heritage of faith and freedom before you become so involved emotionally that it is difficult to think clearly and decide wisely.

Important as all these factors are in considering the path of true love, the most essential one for happiness in marriage is the nature of love itself. It means surrender and sacrifice and self-giving, each putting the other first, and each seeking the other's happiness before his own. It means not getting but giving and giving gladly, only to find that you gain far more than you ever can give. "Love asks for nothing. Everything comes back to it."

Dr. Roy Burkhart in *The Secret of a Happy Marriage* suggests the following questions which are excellent tests of true love:

> Is the most wonderful thought to be with the loved person and the most unhappy thought to be separated from that person?
>
> Are you personally attracted to the loved one? Are you attracted to the physical self? To the mental self? To the social self? To the spiritual self?
>
> Do you feel proud to be with the loved person in the presence of all the people you know?
>
> Do objects or things associated with this person have greater meaning because of him or of her?
>
> As you look over the history of your relationship have you grown in fondness, in mutual interests, in contagion for each other, in freedom of expression with each other, in mutual understanding?
>
> As you consider the question of attraction, does the loved

one call forth a real response? On the other hand, can you truly enjoy being with the loved one without physical sharing and physical expression of your love?

Have you applied the test of time? Ordinarily a couple ought to have at least a year of fellowship and acquaintance and then some months of engagement before marriage.

What is the basis of the attraction? Is it what the person can give you? Or the person's family connection? Or is it the person himself or herself?

How does the loved one compare with others in your own mind? Is he or she supreme?

Is this loved one as vital in your thoughts when absent as when present?

Is this the kind of person you would like to join with in bringing children into the world?

Is the love you feel together great enough to weather the crises and conflicts and the misunderstandings that come as you grow together?

Are your highest ideals shared by the loved one?

Do you share together interests that are worthy of your complete devotion?

If you can answer "Yes" to these questions then your love is certainly the real thing and provides a good basis for marriage.

There are also sins against love of which you must beware. You sin against love if you take advantage of it for your own gain or your own satisfaction. You sin against the deeper meaning of love if your interest is only physical. An increasing desire for physical expression leading up to marriage is right in love, but you do yourself and your love a disservice when you allow this to dominate your relationship.

As you consider different friends as possible life partners, seek to discover the real and hidden characteristics that are not revealed in a casual acquaintance or a few dates. Determine whether the individual's personality will stand up under various situations. Determine whether your two personalities supplement and enrich each other and whether you are so fond of each other that you are willing and eager to give up everybody else. Christian courtship serves such purposes and is always courteous and clean, cautious and constructive. Take a good long look before you leap.

If you want to develop a secure and lasting love, be yourself. Do not pretend to be what you think the other wants you to be, but be your own best self. Spend enough time together without outside distractions to become really well acquainted. Discover your mutual interests and share them and develop new interests together. Do not pretend an interest. True love cannot be built on sham or pretense. Get acquainted with each other's family and friends and see how you get along with them. Be frank with each other as to how soon you will be ready to marry. If necessary, seek the guidance of a reliable marriage counselor or your parents, your pastor, or a trusted friend or teacher.

Test your love by separation when you think you have found the real thing. If yours is true love you will mean all the more to each other when you are together again. Often you hear that "absence makes the heart grow fonder of somebody else." Sometimes that is true, but it may be all to the good. If your love will not stand the test of absence, it probably will not stand the far more important test, the test of presence; that is whether you can actually get along together or whether you will eventually tire of each other.

Can your love stand the test of expression? Is there real self-giving? Are you each earnestly and honestly trying to put the other and the other's happiness first? Can your love stand the test of growth? Only if it grows will you be ready for engagement and then for marriage. Elizabeth Barrett Browning expressed it beautifully in lines that reveal the true meaning of love for her and for countless others:

> How do I love thee? Let me count the ways:
> I love thee to the depth and breadth and height
> My soul can reach, when feeling out of sight
> For the ends of Being and ideal Grace.
> I love thee to the level of everyday's
> Most quiet need, by sun and candlelight.
> I love thee freely, as men strive for Right;
> I love thee purely, as they turn from Praise;
> I love thee with the passion put to use
> In my old griefs, and with my childhood's faith;
> I love thee with a love I seemed to lose
> With my lost saints—I love thee with the breath,
> Smiles, tears, of all my life! And if God choose,
> I shall but love thee better after death.

There's No Place Like a Christian Home

MANY who face the vicissitudes of life from day to day are ready to say half cynically and half humorously with Dagwood of the comic strip, "There's no place like home, absolutely no place." So many things can happen at home and usually do. With all its joys and its sorrows, its pleasure and its pain, its happy hours and its tragic, home is the place where we learn to grow up and meet life's varying challenges and responsibilities.

Christians have learned by experience and can say with joy and gratitude, "There is absolutely no place like a Christian home" for developing manhood and womanhood to the very finest and best, and to assure to a man and woman and their children the highest joys and the deepest satisfactions that life can bring.

The movie *Quo Vadis* is a graphic portrayal of the difference Christian ideals make in the life of a man or woman. The heroine tells the pagan man she loves that he and Christ both have a place in her heart. Because Christ means nothing to him, he says angrily that he will not share that place with anybody else and leaves her. It is only as he finally comes to understand that it is Christ who has made her such a lovely girl that he is willing to share a place in her heart with her Lord.

We are thinking about love and home from the Christian standpoint. Paul in the 13th Chapter of I Corinthians tells us some of the qualities that are essential in human love and which we should cherish as Christians: "Love is very patient, very kind, knows no jealousy, makes no parade, gives itself no airs, is never rude, never selfish, never irritated, never resentful; love is never glad when others go wrong, love is gladdened by goodness, always slow to expose, always eager to believe the best, always hopeful, always patient" [Moffatt]. John tells us in the little letter that we call I John how important it is that our human love be hallowed by the divine love of God. "Love is of God and everyone that loveth is begotten of God and knoweth God, for God is love."

Christian love is sacred and clean. You feel that God has made you for each other and that you share something divine. It is realistic, as we have seen, and has a physical basis, mental ties and emotional qualities that give love its dynamic and power—the power to see it through whatever the cost. The essential spiritual quality leads us to sing as a wedding hymn:

> O perfect love, all human love transcending,
> Lowly we kneel in prayer before thy throne,
> That ours may be the love which knows no ending,
> Whom Thou forevermore hast joined in one.

The evil in life will kill love. The good will help it to live and grow. Paul says, "Let your love be a real thing with a loathing for evil and a bent for good" (Romans 12:9). Thank God for the strength you need to be worthy of it. If there is anything for which you cannot thank God or share with Him, you are better off without it.

Love is frequently thought of largely in terms of sex and often a very low concept at that. The Kinsey Report gives a startling picture of sex behavior in this country. It is not a complete picture, but it does reveal a large percentage of premarital sex relationships and unfaithfulness in marriage. That is not the way of life for one who cherishes the Christian ideal that calls for personal purity, social integrity, and marital fidelity. The Kinsey Report, interestingly enough, points out that religion does make a difference. Among Protestant, Catholic, and Jewish men who had an active church relationship or a vital Christian faith the percentage of those who lived in the right way was far higher than among those who lived without the stabilizing help of religious ideals and associations.

As you face the temptations of life and the problems of marriage with the help of the Lord Christ, you find that you can be true to the vows you take in the wedding service to forsake all others and cleave only to the one to whom you promise all your love and devotion. Only as the two really do become one, not only physically and legally and financially, but also spiritually, have they found the way to that deep and abiding joy that undergirds all Christian married life. Such a joy is known even through pain, for you know that whatever life may bring, with God's help, you two can share it together.

Kenneth I. Brown has written a book entitled *Margie*. It is about one of the finest Christians girls I have known. She wrote to the boy she planned to marry: "I love you not only for what you are but for what I am when I am with you. I love you not only for what you have made of yourself but for what you are making of me. You have done it without a touch, without a word, without a sign; you have done it by being yourself. I guess that is what being a sweetheart really means."

That is Christian love at its highest and best. From such a love can come the Christian homes Jesus portrayed as God's unit of society and man's hope for a better world.

In *Wind, Sand, and Stars* Antoine de Saint Exupéry wrote the beautiful words, "Life has taught us that love does not consist in gazing at each other, but in looking outward together in the same direction. There is no comradeship except from union in the same high effort. That is the building of a Christian home."

Such a home has come to a lovely Christian couple who visited me again some years after I had married them. Their two children were with them. As we sat talking in my study, the children seated on their parents' laps, I looked at the mother and said, "I remember the day you sat in that chair when we were arranging for your wedding." She smiled as she remembered too. We talked for some time about all that love and marriage had brought to them, how their love had stood the test of absence during the war years, had drawn them even closer when they could be together again, and had grown to provide a happy home for the four of them.

Now they told me they faced another time of separation because his service called him overseas. They had love enough for it all, however, and I knew the reason. Back in the days when they were becoming serious with each other she was a Christian and he was not. That other day when we had talked about the arrangements for their wedding, I had said, "Now what about your church home?" He answered, "I am going to accept Christ and join the church before we marry." The following Sunday he came and publicly acknowledged Christ as his Saviour and Lord. We baptized him and later they were married and went on their way with a consciousness of the love of God blessing and hallowing their life together.

Before they left again we went once more into the sanctuary to pray and ask God to bless them. Such love is real. It will always stand the test of time. All who would build enduring homes will do well to pray with Daniel Henderson in his lovely "Hymn for a Household":

> Lord Christ, beneath thy starry dome,
> We light this flickering lamp of home,
> And where bewildering shadows throng,
> Uplift our prayer and evensong.
> Dost thou, with heaven in thy ken,
> Seek still a dwelling place with men,
> Wandering the world in ceaseless quest?
> O Man of Nazareth, be our guest!
>
> Lord Christ, the bird his nest has found,
> The fox is sheltered in his ground,
> But dost thou still this dark earth tread
> And have no place to lay thy head?
> Shepherd of mortals, here behold
> A little flock, a wayside fold
> That wait thy presence to be blest—
> O Man of Nazareth, be our guest!

We should remember that as Christians we must be as concerned for the homes and lives and happiness of all God's children as for our own. In such a world as ours other homes will touch and influence the homes of our loved ones in countless ways. We are all "bound in the bundle of life" and have been told, "Bear ye one another's burdens and so fulfill the law of Christ" (Galatians 6:2). The attitudes and ideals that are nurtured in your home and passed on to the next generation will help determine the kind of world in which tomorrow's homes are to be built. We are but a part of the family of God on earth.

It is time for us as Christians to rethink old prejudices that have counted others of God's children as inferior and beneath us, forgetting that "He hath made of one blood all nations to dwell on the face of the earth" (Acts 17:26). Recognizing the differences of background and culture, let us teach our children to respect all other races and nations for what they are and other individuals as persons whatever their color or creed. Let us seek to substitute knowledge for ignorance, understanding for prejudice, love for hate, brotherhood for strife, justice for injustice, looking toward the day of Christian fellowship and good will between all those for whom Christ died. Did he not say, "This is my commandment, That ye love one another, as I have loved you" (John 15:12)?

Poverty, insecurity, insufficient food and clothing, inadequate shelter and education anywhere must be our concern as Christians. We dare not seek in God's name any blessings for our own lives and homes that we do not seek for others. Jesus said, "Inasmuch as ye have done it unto the least of these, my brethren, ye have done it unto me" (Matthew 25:40). His universal love and concern for his brethren must be ours. Only then is there hope that all the homes of tomorrow can be his and that our own homes can endure.

War and hate challenge the very existence of our homes. The parents of today are rearing the generation that must win the peace of tomorrow. Since the Christian homes of today are our best hope for a better tomorrow, we must give our children

Jesus' ideals of world redemption and world brotherhood. No couple can ever do this alone. Each of our homes must be reinforced by a church home where our children will be taught the Word of God and given a faith in God that will fit them for the coming days. "The Christian Church," someone has truly said, "is always within one generation of extinction." It must win the next generation.

To that end make religion natural in your home. Prayers at bedtime, the blessing at the table, some form of devotion and Bible reading should have a place in the daily program. Lead the children naturally to the day when they will make their own decision for Christ and the church. It is folly for you to neglect all this, saying that they will eventually decide their religion for themselves. True, the ultimate choice is theirs. No one can choose Christ as Lord for someone else. But yours is the responsibility of giving them the religious training and atmosphere that ultimately lead to that all-important decision.

A recent writer says that in all modern arguments about religion he cannot forget seeing his father kneel to pray at night before he went to bed. "My father prayed." What a help that is in guiding life. Yet thousands of children today have never seen nor heard their father or mother pray. This matter of a family faith and a church home is more important than many realize. The eminent psychologist Dr. Henry C. Link states in his book, *The Return to Religion,* that he found himself advising so many other people to go back to church he finally decided he should do so himself. He tells how this brought him genuine satisfaction and then goes on to point out that fine personalities in children are developed, first, when the children attend Sunday School, and second, when the parents go to church. From such homes, he says, come the poised and self-reliant leaders of society.

In your hands also rests the married happiness and well-being of the next generation. You largely determine the child's attitudes, habits, ideals, and expectations. You are the ones who, with the help of the church and the school, must develop in the next generation, the fathers and mothers of tomorrow, such qualities as integrity, restraint, honor, concern for others, brotherhood and good will. You must teach them by word and deed a sense of fair play, the ability to face difficulties with a smile, and to get their own way by fair means or not at all. All of these qualities will be needed in the homes of tomorrow, and they must be taught and caught in the homes of today. Who of us is great enough alone for such a responsibility? Wise are the parents who take God's help in it all.

One of the leading ministers of his day paid this tribute to his boyhood home, "The things that make for happiness in the home are the things that make for happiness everywhere, only more so, because the home is the most profound of all human relationships. There we give and forgive, bear and forbear, and so learn the fine art of living together. It is in the home that we are emotionally conditioned. That decides what we are to be, whether we are to live by faith or by fear."

He goes on to say, "If I am a minister of religion, it is because my mother was one who lived by faith and prayer. My earliest memory of her is hearing her pray, hearing my name in her prayer when she did not know I heard. She lifted my little life on the wings of prayer and gave it to God and that consecration abides."

What are you going to give your children for their tomorrow? What will you build into their lives that will endure? What memories will they cherish of you and your home that will guide their lives aright come what may? Dare you give them less than the highest? Give them above all else love at its best, your own love, the love of Christ, the love of God and all that is good.

John H. Styles, Jr. reflects in "My Altar":

> I have worshipped in churches and chapels;
> I've prayed in the busy street;
> I have sought my God and have found him
> Where the waves of the ocean beat;
> I have knelt in the silent forest
> In the shade of some ancient tree;
> But the dearest of all my altars
> Was raised at my mother's knee.
>
> I have listened to God in his temple;
> I've caught his voice in the crowd;
> I have heard him speak when the breakers
> Were booming long and loud;
> Where the winds play soft in the treetops
> My father has talked to me;
> But I never have heard him clearer
> Than I did at my mother's knee.
>
> The things in my life that are worthy
> Were born in my mother's breast,
> And breathed into mine by the magic
> Of the love her life expressed.
> The years that have brought me to manhood
> Have taken her far from me;
> But memory keeps me from straying
> Too far from my mother's knee.

God, make me the man of her vision
And purge me of selfishness!
God, keep me true to her standards
And help me to live and to bless!
God, hallow the holy impress
Of the days that used to be,
And keep me a pilgrim forever
To that shrine at my mother's knee.

Do you remember the story in *Folkhouse* by Mary E. Waller? Martin and Ann fall in love while they are in college. For a time marriage seems impossible, but when he is appointed to the faculty as an instructor they find an office in an old abandoned mill nearby which they can convert into a one-room apartment. As his salary goes up and the family increases, they take over more and more of the old mill for their home. Since all of their parents are dead, they adopt a lonely old lady as their grandmother, and the three generations live on happily until World War I.

Then Martin goes to war. After hostilities have ceased for some time Ann begins to wonder why he has not returned. His letters are strange and he is so indefinite about his plans. Finally she learns that when Martin does come home he will be blind. He has delayed his return until he has mastered Braille so that he can carry on his work in the university.

When the great day comes the old family doctor says to Ann, "Martin is coming home. I'll meet him at the train and bring him to you, for when he comes he wants not your pity but your strength and your love." As Martin stands again at the door of the old mill, Ann and the children rush to throw their arms around him to take him back into their hearts and their home. The old grandmother sitting by the fire says, "Who shall separate us from the love of Christ? Shall nakedness, or peril, or sword, or famine, or things present, or things to come, or height, or depth, or any other creature? Nay, in all these things we are more than conquerors through Him who loved us" (Romans 8:35).

Such homes built on the rock of faith will live and live forever. They have an eternal quality only the Christian faith can give.

Hartzell Spence tells of the last time he saw his father alive. The old minister who has served his Lord well is nearing the end of life's journey. The son must leave at once to accept a new job, and they both know they will never see each other again. The minister takes the boy's hands and says, "Son, I am very happy over your promotion. I like to be proud of my sons. You are going far away. When you return, I probably will not be here. But don't worry about me. We are both moving up to new jobs. You know you are going to New York, and just as surely I know where I am going. You know what to expect when you get there, and so do I." He looks at him steadily for a moment and says, "God bless you, son. Goodbye."

What a faith to have and to give! Is it yours? You can have it through Christ, and your love and your home can be all God meant them to be.

VI

So You Are Engaged

S OMEONE has said, "Life is one crazy thing after another, and love is two crazy things after each other." However crazy lovers may seem sometimes, if their affection is genuine they will eventually become engaged. This is a significant and important time of life. The young lady will go around shaking hands with her left hand, and the man will beam with joy as the ring sparkles in the light, the ring that says they are pledged to each other for life.

A good engagement is usually the prelude to a good marriage. There would be fewer unhappy marriages if couples took more time for their engagement. Those who study success and failure in marriage tell us that the average engagement should be from six months to two years. A longer period creates problems of its own, but six months is none too long when so much is to be accomplished by those who are really to succeed in marriage. A longer courtship, of course, makes possible a shorter engagement.

This thrilling time is quite a different experience from courtship. The two begin to plan their lives together. Others are forgotten and they think only of each other and of their future. It is a time of testing, of preparation, of growing understanding and intimacy. It is a time of personality adjustment when they begin to rub off the rough edges that irritate each other. They learn the little habits that annoy and stop them, and speak more freely than during courtship of the things that might contribute to or mar their mutual happiness. It is a time of growing understanding of each other's interests, and when they add to their common store of activities and friends. They get acquainted with each other's families and seek their approval and blessing. Many marriages fail or are unhappy because the couple in their first months together must make the adjustments that should have been effected during courtship and engagement.

One woman, for example, whose marriage was in imminent danger of breaking up, came to understand that her difficulty really was caused by too short an engagement. The man she married had been torn between her and another woman and did not know which one he really loved, if he loved either one. Foolishly she rushed into marriage, only to find the other woman still very much in the picture and her marriage doomed to almost certain failure. The husband never was able to make his choice between the two and the wife eventually had to leave an unbearable situation. A longer engagement would have revealed the true situation and saved much of heartache and embarrassment.

Although engagement does bring a growing intimacy and a deepening love, keep for marriage and marriage only the physical expressions of love that should follow your wedding. Many an engagement has failed to issue in marriage because of weakness at this point, and many a marriage has been handicapped because of doubts about each other that root back in premarital sex relationships.

During engagement the couple settle the date and time of the wedding, the kind of ceremony, the place to spend the honeymoon, and the housekeeping arrangements. It is a time when the man saves his money and adds to his insurance, and the woman adds to her "hope chest." She develops the skills of cooking, sewing, and homemaking. Husbands have often asked, "How can I get my wife to learn to cook?" Any woman who expects to make a home ought to fit herself for that responsibility as surely as she learns her shorthand or develops other skills that enable her to support herself alone.

Gates Hebbard gives this "Advice for Grooms-to-Be":

> Gentlemen, before you wed
> Ascertain how you'll be fed.
> Delve into each pan and pot
> That your bride-to-be has got.
> Though her kisses always please,
> What about her recipes?
> Though her glamour makes you sigh
> Can she bake an apple pie?
> Now, before it is too late,
> Learn your gastronomic fate.
> Do not trust your burning ardor
> Till you've snooped around her larder.
> More than once has sex appeal
> Died with that initial meal.

As you think of engagement ask yourself the following questions. If you do not qualify on some of these points, face the fact frankly and make any necessary adjustments in yourself and in your thinking or your marriage may suffer.

Are your parents happily married? If they are, you have a very real chance of success in marriage. If your parents are not happily married, then you should be careful lest you carry over into your marriage any attitudes caused by their unhappiness that might hurt your own.

Did you have a happy childhood? Happiness in childhood helps to create the kind of personality that can be happy and successful in marriage. If you were not, then you should take an honest look at yourself to be sure that your attitudes toward others have not been marred by your own unhappiness.

Were you free from conflict with your mother? That does not mean that your mother never corrected you. It does mean that there was a basic understanding between you and your mother and you did have a strong attachment to her. Did you have a strong attachment to your father? If so, it augurs well for your marriage. Were your parents firm and fair in their discipline, but not harsh or cruel? If so, it should mean that you are self-controlled and able to discipline yourself and others.

Were your parents frank with you about sex? An early and adequate understanding of the place of sex in life helps greatly in sexual adjustment and in your attitude toward your life partner. Is your own attitude toward sex free from disgust and aversion? If not, by all means seek a counselor who can help you understand sex as God meant it to be. Were you taught that there is something inherently wrong or unclean about the sex relationship? If you were, then you have not learned the truth about it as yet. God created sex and anything that He created for us is clean and wholesome, sacred and beautiful, when rightly understood and used. Sex can be low and debased, to be sure, but it need not be. If you are going into marriage without an adequate understanding of God's truth about sex, then you are not really ready for marriage. Doctors, pastors, and marriage counselors are ready to help you about this and other problems.

You will, of course, consider the coming of children and whether you want them as soon as possible. As a rule it is better for a young couple to have a year of adjustment together before starting a family. Children should come into this world because they are wanted and planned for. Foolish are those who selfishly delay too long the coming of children or who plan to have no children, if it is at all possible to have them. Go to your doctor for a good physical examination, talk with him frankly about your sex relationship, and get from him the information you will need about birth control and planned parenthood.

You should settle where you are going to live. Much trouble will be avoided if you have a place of your own, small though it may be. It may not be as luxurious as you would like. It may not be in the location you would prefer, but if it is yours alone that is the important thing. Decide whether the girl is to continue working in her job as well as at home. You will want to talk frankly about what you have to live on, what you are going to save, and the financial goals toward which you are going to strive.

Much of your thought will be given to the wedding itself. Talk frankly about the expense involved so that you will not spend too much on the ceremony but only enough to make it memorable and distinctive and particularly yours. Do not think you must do certain things just because somebody else did but plan to do whatever will make the day a beautiful and fitting one for you.

During engagement doubts sometimes arise in the minds of one or both. Face such questions together or with a trusted counselor. You do want to satisfy yourselves that you are well mated and that God has made you for each other. If you are troubled on this score or want some reassurance, here are some questions that you might ask. They come from the helpful book by Clifford R. Adams entitled *How to Pick a Mate*. To the questions I have added some comments of my own.

Are you two equally sociable? That is, are you both gad-abouts or stay-at-homes? Are your social desires about alike?

Are you both stern-minded with strict and rigid standards, or are you both broad-minded and adjustable? Are you two of a kind? Opposites may attract each other, but similarities make for happiness in the home.

Does he find satisfaction and reward in his work, and do you like housework? Happiness and security in one's job are important, and the housework does have to be done so you might as well learn to enjoy doing it and doing it well.

Are you both over 20 and under 40? As a rule is is better to be over 20 than under, for most teen-age marriages have a hard time and many of them fail. Whatever your age, are you near enough in age and maturity to be congenial?

Is he regarded by his acquaintances as a fairly dependable person not given to excuse making and little sly lies?

Has your dating been steady for a year or more and been relatively free from quarrels? Of course, there will be some misunderstandings, but you will make up and love each other all the more afterward. However, you don't want that to happen too often. If it does, are you sure you really know each other and are basically suited for each other?

Do you have about the same religious beliefs and attitudes? Have you settled where you are to worship and make a church home together?

Do both sets of parents favor the marriage? Certainly you know each other's families and have sought their approval and blessing.

Are you in good physical health? Each should have a complete physical examination before marriage.

Do you both have about the same emotional responsiveness and warmth of passion and feeling? Is there anything about the other that is irritating or repulsive to you? If so, talk about it frankly and kindly before marriage.

Are you free of jealousy and suspicion? Do you trust each other fully and completely?

Does he have a calm, even temperament, especially if you are one to fly off the handle quickly and vice versa?

Do you both have a healthy attitude toward sex? It will be helpful for both of you to read at least one or two good books about the sex relationship. You will find a number of them listed in the appendix.

Are you both temperate in your habits? Increasing alcoholism among women as well as men is a serious threat to the American home.

Do you both feel very deeply that God has made you for each other? Have you learned to pray together about your problems as well as to talk about them?

To get the voice of experience on some of these problems the young married couples in our church were asked to tell us what adjustments were most difficult and most essential in the early months of married life and what counsel they would give those who are looking toward marriage.

The young wives said they had found they needed understanding, patience, a Christian faith, love, honesty, a sense of humor, thrift, unselfishness, faithfulness, thoughtfulness. They emphasized the importance of having a flexible nature, a willingness to learn, a willingness to forgive and forget, controlled emotions, and an open mind. One wife very honestly said, "I had to learn that my husband had a mind of his own and that my every wish was not his command."

When asked to turn the spotlight on themselves the young husbands said they had found these qualities essential to be a good husband: a Christian, understanding and patience, a sense of humor, faithfulness, education, character, loyalty, a homemaker, unselfishness and ability to provide the necessities of life.

If during engagement you find that you do not really belong to each other or if you have deep and serious doubts about your chances for success, you ought not to marry. There is nothing dishonorable about ending the relationship. You are pledged to seek the best for each other. Many who have thought they were in love, and perhaps were for a time, find when they take enough time together that they do not have a good basis for marriage. Though hearts may be broken or feelings hurt for awhile, it is far better to face up to your mistake before marriage than after.

It is usually customary for the girl to announce that she has broken the engagement, even though the man may be the one who feels he cannot marry her. This courtesy grows out of the very real fact that the man then is free to look for somebody else, but the girl has to wait for somebody to seek her.

If you are worried about whether you will ever marry, take courage from the fact that the percentage of men over fourteen years of age who are unmarried in this country decreased from 35 per cent in 1940 to 26 per cent in 1949. The percentage of unmarried women over fourteen dropped from 28 per cent in 1940 to only 20 per cent in 1949. Thus in the United States today only about one fourth of the men and one fifth of the women over fourteen are unmarried. This trend indicates that nearly all those who want to marry will eventually have a home of their own.

Three key words, faith, hope, and love, sum up our thought thus far. Faith in God and in each other is essential, an assurance that God has made you for each other and that as you face life with Him there is nothing the years can bring that will be too great for the three of you.

> Live not without your God;
> However low or high,
> In every house should be
> A window to the sky.

Hope—hope that is not just visionary or based on mere dreams and illusions, but hope that is built on knowledge, knowledge of each other, knowledge about the facts of life and sex and marriage. A hope that is built on an understanding of the ways and moods, the likes and dislikes, the hopes and dreams of each other. This will come to you as you grow and grow together and seek the guidance of God in all your plans and problems.

Faith, hope, and love—for without love you never can be happy. With love you can endure almost anything if you face it honestly and together. True love is the magic key that opens the door to the best that engagement and marriage can bring.

There is a beautiful story behind one of the oldest French Huguenot families of Virginia. Some of the Huguenots came to this country years ago for refuge from persecution. Others went to England and the Netherlands. In England the young man in one family fell in love with an English servant. Since she did not come from a wealthy and educated family, the French father felt that she was not good enough for his boy.

He thought he would solve the problem by sending the boy to the new land of America.

The young man grew and prospered here, for he was able and industrious. He needed a servant in his home, and when he heard that a shipment of English servants was being docked on a certain day, he went down prepared to pay the passage cost of someone who would then be his servant for a period of years. As he looked up on the deck of the ship he saw standing there the girl he loved. The moment they could get together they fell into each other's arms. He asked, "Why did you come?" but his question was unnecessary. She replied, "I came because I love you." He told her that he loved her still and had never loved another. So it was her passage that he paid, and it was to their home that he took her, a home that was built on faith and hope and love, a home from which came one of the finest families of Virginia.

Still another young couple faced an extraordinary test of their love. He was a young minister; she a lovely Christian girl in his church. Their engagement was announced and the wedding day set. Then one day in an accident he broke his neck and was paralyzed from the shoulders down. He offered to release her, but her affection and devotion would not let him go. She nursed him and watched over him as he slowly regained his health and strength. Each inspired and upheld the other until he was strong enough to carry on a measure of his work. The day finally arrived when they could be married. She walked down the aisle on her father's arm. He came down another aisle in his wheel chair, pushed by one of his minister friends. Before God and their loved ones they took their vows so long delayed, yet filled with more meaning than ever because they had proved the strength of their love in the face of trial. The service was one they had written themselves, but at its heart were words whose truth they had demonstrated and a promise they had proved they could keep. "And now abideth faith, hope and love, these three, and the greatest of these is love."

"Whatsoever things are pure and true and honest and lovely and of good report, think on these things" (Philippians 4:8), and in God's good way and time in spite of everything, your dreams of marriage and home can come true.

Chapter

VII

No Longer Two But One

STORYBOOKS often say, "And they lived happily forever after." That may be the storybook ending, but the wedding is really just the beginning. How can the couple who are "no longer two but one" realize fully the hopes and dreams of their wedding day?

That day, with all its sacred rites and beautiful symbolism, is above all else the bride's day. Of course, there are some cynics who say, "This is a woman's world anyway. When a man is born into the world the first question people ask is, 'How is his mother?' When he is married, they ask, 'How did the bride look?' When he dies, they want to know 'How much did he leave her?' It's a woman's world!"

When all is said and done, there is no higher or finer hour in the life of a young man and young woman than when they stand before God and their loved ones and, before a minister of Jesus Christ, pledge themselves to the high adventure of sharing life with each other in marriage forever after. Forever is a long time, and those who take such vows and start a new home are committed to a total and eternal union. That is what Jesus taught as he gave us the Christian ideal of marriage. "They are no longer two but one. What therefore God

hath joined together, let not man put asunder" (Matthew
19:6).

All too often very little thought is given to the wedding itself, though sometimes just the opposite is true and the couple
are so worn out on their wedding day that they are unable to
enjoy or appreciate it. They start on their honeymoon ex-
hausted and unfit for a happy entrance into the joys of married life. At the other extreme, some couples will call up the
minister in the morning and ask him if he is too busy to marry
them that night. What a poor idea of marriage that is! Take
plenty of time in advance to make arrangements. Go together
to talk with your pastor and seek his guidance and counsel. If
you belong to different churches it is usually customary for the
bride's pastor to conduct the service, though another minister
may assist him. The arrangements ought to be made early both
with him and with the church, the florist, musicians, and
others.

The groom needs to learn that it is the bride who attends
to most of the details. She determines the date, the place, the
preacher, and the kind of wedding it will be. The groom just
determines to be there and make the best of it. It is her day,
and wise is the man who decides to help make it as happy and
meaningful as possible for the one he loves.

The wedding should be in keeping with your circumstances.
It does not have to be a big church wedding with a vast ex-
penditure of money to make it memorable. It should be in
keeping with your personalities, your income, and the conditions in your family. It should be, not someone else's wedding,
but your own. Let it be, not a secret affair, but one to which
your families and your friends are invited to share with you
in one of the most significant hours in all of life.

It ought, of course, to be a religious ceremony in which you stand together as your minister asks God's blessing on your relationship. In that sacred hour he will read from God's Word and remind you of the eternal significance of marriage. He will say first to the groom and then to the bride, "Do you take the one you love and whose hand you hold to be your lawful and wedded wife, and do you promise to love, cherish, honor, and sustain her in sickness or in health, for better for worse, for richer for poorer, so long as ye both shall live?" What a promise that is! One not to be made lightly. You sense then, as never before, why it takes time to get ready for such a sacred covenant and lasting responsibility.

With the giving and receiving of the rings, the couple make such a covenant as this, "With this ring I wed thee, giving thee my heart's best love." From that day on each comes first in the other's life. When the minister asks God's blessing on your life and love together, pronounces you husband and wife, and says, "What God hath joined together, let not man put asunder," you are married for time and for eternity.

As you get ready, it may well be that you are troubled because of some sin in the past. You may ask yourself whether you are worthy of her love, or of his. Often individuals are faced with that problem and wonder whether or not they should confess to the one they love sins and mistakes of earlier days. If, of course, it is to be known anyway, your life partner ought to learn it from you. As a rule, however, it is much better for you to be accepted for what you are without bringing up again sins and shortcomings that have long since been confessed to God, forgiven, and forgotten. If through faith you have found forgiveness and peace in your own mind and heart, you can come to your wedding altar feeling that through

Jesus Christ the past has been washed away and you are bringing pure love and a true purpose to your marriage. Claim for yourself the promise, "As far as the East is from the West, so far hath He removed our transgressions from us" (Psalm 103:12), and go ahead in faith to build a new life with the one you love.

Many have had an experience similar to that of one boy who wanted to marry a lovely Christian girl. He knew in his heart he was not worthy of her, but with deep conviction and sincerity he accepted Christ as his Saviour and began life over again as a different man with new strength and new determination. He has made a fine husband and father because he started right through faith in Jesus Christ, and she loved and accepted him as the man Christ had helped him to become.

You need such a faith if you are to be ready for marriage, ready for that day when you and your beloved will stand before a sacred altar, sacred not only because God is there, but also because He is at home in your hearts and will be enshrined in your home. As you clasp your hands and bow your heads for the benediction and leave that altar to begin your life together, blessed is the bride to whom her husband can say:

> Grow old along with me, the best is yet to be,
> The last of life for which the first was made.
> Our times are in his hand who said a whole I planned,
> Youth shows but half; trust God, see all, nor be afraid.

Every wedding calls for an appropriate and happy honeymoon. As you make your plans bear in mind the purpose of those first happy hours together. Be sure you have time for adjustment and for relaxation after the strain of the days before the wedding. It need not be long, but it should give a couple time alone to make the adjustments those early days will bring and to make the transition to married ways of life. So many make the mistake of thinking they must rush from place to place and cover as much territory as possible, or see all the friends they can visit, or go to some fashionable spot and spend a lot of money. That is unnecessary. A honeymoon should be a time when you two, and you two alone, really begin to learn to live together. Make your plans to suit your own needs, temperaments and pocketbooks, and then with some happy memories and new bonds of love get back to work and the big job of building the home of your dreams.

It is important as you start married life together to understand the difference in the attitudes and desires of men and women. In *Preparing for Marriage* Clifford R. Adams reports that in a recent study a group of single men and single women were asked to list in order the things that they were seeking in marriage. We are not talking now about the qualities that they are seeking in the person they marry, but the basic desires in themselves that would lead them to marry. Both men and women wanted practically the same things but in quite a different order. The men gave as their basic desires companionship, 40 per cent; sexual satisfaction, 30 per cent; love, 15 per cent; children, 10 per cent; home, 5 per cent. With the women the order was: love, 33 per cent; security, 27 per cent; companionship, 20 per cent; children, 11 per cent; sexual satisfaction, 9 per cent.

Now when two people come together with such basic desires and yet in such a different order of importance you can see how essential it is that you understand each other and are concerned for the other's desires and greatest good. Only through patience and love can both husband and wife be fully satisfied and happy.

This is one reason why it is so important that the two be Christian. If, for example, the man is moved largely by a desire for sexual gratification, and the woman comes out of a sheltered background, very much in love with him, but with very little sexual desire at the moment, they face a difficult adjustment unless both are Christian. If you are to make this and other adjustments, you must be patient and willing to wait for some of your desires to be fully realized and for a complete understanding between you. Married happiness can and will be achieved as sex desires are both awakened and disciplined and love and comradeship grow.

A satisfactory sex adjustment depends, first of all, on knowledge of the physical and emotional facts about life and about each other. Much of the difficulty here roots in selfishness or in fear, fear that in turn stems from ignorance or false ideas.

The knowledge and acceptance of certain basic facts will help in an early and satisfactory sex adjustment. Further physical details and helpful suggestions will be found in the specialized books and pamphlets listed in the bibliography. The following facts should be understood by both husband and wife:

> The sex relationship is a normal and proper part of married life and should be approached intelligently and anticipated eagerly and without fear by both husband and wife.
>
> Satisfactory relationships can be achieved by any normal couple, though the first attempts may be awkward, and for the woman, slightly painful.
>
> The act of intercourse should be preceded by a period of preparation, with kissing, fondling, and expressions of

endearment until both husband and wife are ready, it usually taking longer for the woman than the man to be fully aroused.

The actual time of intercourse is usually relatively brief and should be followed by a sense of satisfaction and togetherness on the part of both husband and wife.

To this end, the wife as well as the husband should ordinarily experience an orgasm or climax with its consequent release of tension. For some women this experience comes more slowly and less frequently and fully than for others, but it is possible for most women. The husband should always be alert to see that the wife is satisfied as well as himself, if she desires it.

Intercourse is not only for the procreation of children. It is also a means of pleasure and the expression of affection for husband and wife; hence it is important that every couple obtain from their physician or other reputable sources adequate information with reference to birth control.

The frequency of intercourse will vary with the couple and with age and circumstances. Each partner should be eager to consider the other's needs and wishes, with due regard for varying moods, weariness, illness, and family responsibilities.

The sex relationship should not become routine, or a mere matter of duty or necessity. Let it always be an expression of love, though intensity of feeling may vary. Variety in the time and in the positions for intercourse help in keeping the relationship at its best.

Most couples experience some delay at first in achieving a satisfying relationship. This may be due to nervousness, tension, weariness, or other emotional or physical factors. Usually patience and consideration and a little time are all that are required for successful intercourse. If further difficulty is experienced the couple should consult a physician for help and counsel.

I think of one couple who have gone on to a very happy married life, for whom the early months of marriage were a bitter and disillusioning experience. In time the counsel of a wise doctor, plus the love and determination of the two, opened the way to a satisfactory adjustment. They have been very happy together and now have a fine family. It can be done if you remember that God created you to live together as husband and wife.

A well-adjusted, happy marriage is just as happy and well-adjusted as the two partners are within themselves and with each other and no more. It is important, then, as you begin your home not only to say and do the right thing, but to do it in the right spirit and for the good of your partner and your new relationship. Someone has truly said, "Love is not only an emotional feeling, it is also an intellectual discipline." A young wife who has learned this says, "In choosing a husband I believe the prime factor would be to consider whether we had the same basic ideals and philosophy. In other words, the two of us would have to be in agreement about the things that matter most. If, for instance, he put financial security at the top of his list and I put religion there, it would be a constant tug of war and tension between us and our marriage would probably end in an unholy deadlock instead of a holy wedlock."

When you enter your new home and life begins all over again, there often are times of tension and disillusionment that bring dismay and disappointment. Sometimes, of course, marriage is not all people expect because they expect the wrong things. They have thought of marriage as a romantic journey of moonlight and roses, a perpetual courtship plus the pleasures of sex, with absolute freedom and no restraints.

Sooner or later they must come face to face with the stern realities of life and work.

Sometimes people expect that the wedding itself will work miracles and that after the ceremony a person will somehow be different. The minister who marries you does not pronounce any words of magic that miraculously change the man or the woman. By and large they are going to be much the same people after marriage that they were before.

One rock on which couples sometimes get wrecked right at the start is the rock of extravagance. When young people start out thinking they are going to begin on the very scale of life to which one or both have been accustomed, they forget that father and mother have worked through long years to obtain the comfort they now enjoy. You miss much of the fun of marriage if you are not willing to start where you are with what you have and what you can really call your own. You miss some of the real joy of home building unless every new piece of furniture is an event. Much of the joy of acquiring things is in looking forward to them and in saving until you can afford to have them. Your expense budget usually should be based on his salary alone no matter what the wife earns, lest you start on a scale of living you cannot maintain. What she brings in should go into capital investments or savings. You should both have some money that is your very own to spend. It may not be much, but it is yours to spend without accounting to the other. Start right in the use of your money and you will avoid many of the difficulties others face.

They're planning to get married, and I'm rather glad they are.
Although the road ahead today seems difficult and far.
They've very little money, and I'm rather pleased at that;
They'll know the joy of striving in an inexpensive flat.

They're launching out together with high hopes and courage great.
They'd dreamed of having riches, but they've chosen not to wait.
And they're starting out with little—just his salary every week,
And they'll have to save and struggle now for every joy they seek.

Their bills will give them trouble, and they'll sigh for things in vain
She's going to do the cooking, and I fancy 'twill be plain.
He'll help her in the kitchen, and he'll dry the dishes too,
And learn a lot of duties which he never thought he'd do.

But every chair they purchase will be laden with delight;
Every trinket toiled and saved for will with joy be doubly bright.
So I'm not the least bit sorry, but am positively glad
For they'll know the fun of striving which their Dad and Mother had.

Often couples run up against the rock of family attachments, and sometimes it is quite a rock unless you remember that when you married you married the family. Many a person has been greatly blessed by the parents and family of the one he loves. I remember the wise mother-in-law who had to choose a home for her son and his wife who were moving to the city in which she lived. When she told me about the house she had rented for them I said, "Well, that is quite a distance from where you live." "Yes," she replied, "it's a good safe mother-in-law distance." She was a very wise woman.

By contrast with that home which was so happy, I am reminded of another where the wife insisted that she must live right next door to her mother. When she was not in her mother's house, the mother was in hers. She had a telephone by her bed and the first thing she did in the morning and the last thing at night was to talk with her mother. Her husband never really had first place in her life, and theirs was a hard and tragic experience that ended in divorce.

You do owe a very real and continuing obligation to your parents, but you have a primary responsibility to each other. With understanding, consideration, respect, and love you can stand together on this matter.

It is easy to be misled by the troubles of a comparatively small number and to forget that in our thirty-five million homes there are literally millions of couples who thank God day and night for in-laws who love them and help them and who have been a blessing through all the years of their married life.

The problem is more difficult if the parents interfere in the personal affairs of the new couple, or if the wife has never really left her parents or the son is still tied to his mother's apron strings. The old folks simply have to face the fact that they must not intrude in the new home. The two young people will make mistakes, but they learn that way. They need a chance to be independent, and it is far better for them to live by themselves. Parents must give them up and let them make their own way or run the risk of ruining their happiness.

The young couple must agree on what their attitude will be toward the two families and then stick together on that attitude. Be sympathetic with your elders, for there is much that the older folks can teach you, and try to remember that most of what they do and say grows out of genuine love and concern for your best good.

If it is not possible for the newlyweds to live alone there should be in advance a definite understanding with those whose house they share about the responsibilities and the bills, about whose home it is, and any other personal matter that could be a source of difficulty. If possible, however, live by yourselves and have your own home.

The A-B-C of the in-law problem is really this, that you resolve that whatever the test or difficulty you will Always Be Christian. Such an attitude will solve most of these problems. If not, at least you will have peace and integrity in your own heart and the assurance that you have done your best to maintain a right relationship.

The scripture story of Naomi and Ruth, mother-in-law and daughter-in-law, gives one of the most beautiful pictures of love and devotion to be found in all literature. Each person who marries would do well to say in the immortal words of Ruth, "Entreat me not to leave thee, or to turn from following after thee, for whither thou goest, I will go, and where thou lodgest, I will lodge; thy people shall be my people, and thy God my God" (Ruth 1:16).

The Christian who has married a Christian and is determined to build a Christian home will find that marriage is far more than had been expected. It is hard to believe that love can possibly be any more wonderful than it is now, but that really is true. As you set out deliberately to develop new and common interests beyond yourselves, to find new things you can do together, new interests in the community and in the church, as well as in the home, you will grow closer to each other.

It is well to remember that you are not always going to agree and that learning how to differ is one of the secrets of happiness in marriage. Learn to talk things over quietly and reasonably. Learn to respect the other's opinions and ideas, even though you do not agree with them or think they are crazy or foolish. Agree to differ, but resolve to love. If one gets angry, let the other keep cool. If you cannot keep cool, go out where it is cool, but do not "hit and run." When you are wrong, learn to say you are sorry, and be sure you are equally willing either to ask forgiveness or to forgive and forget. "Let not the sun go down upon your wrath." Do not store up bitterness or ill will in your heart, but speak out and then close the day with an understanding and a prayer and an expression of your love for each other. Begin each day with a prayer together asking God's blessing and guidance as you face the day and its demands. To learn all that is to learn how to have the finest fellowship marriage can give.

Robert Louis Stevenson voices the kind of prayer every couple needs to pray from time to time. "We thank Thee for this place in which we dwell, for the love that unites us, for the peace accorded to us this day, for the hope with which we expect the morrow, for the health, the work, the food, and the bright skies that make our life delightful; for our friends in all parts of the earth. Spare to us our friends, soften us to our enemies. Bless us, if it may be, in all our innocent endeavors; if it may not, give us strength to encounter that which is to come, that we may be brave in peril, constant in tribulation, temperate in wrath and in all changes of fortune, and down to the gates of death, loyal and loving one another."

Someone once handed me an old sermonette by a Dr. Holland. I do not know who Dr. Holland was, but he has some very good suggestions for those who are starting their life together.

> Never both be angry at once.
> Never taunt the other with a past mistake.
> Never forget the happy hours of early love.
> Never meet without a loving welcome.
> Never talk *at* each other either alone or in a crowd.

Never yell at each other unless the house is on fire.

Let each one strive oftenest to yield to the wishes of the other.

Let self-denial be the daily aim and practice of each.

Never let the sun go down upon any anger or grievance.

Never allow a reasonable request to have to be made a second time.

Never make a remark in public at the expense of the other. It may seem very funny sometimes, but it hurts.

Never sigh for what might have been, but make the best of what is.

Never find fault unless it is certain that a fault has been committed, and even then, always speak lovingly.

Never part for the day without loving words to think about during the absence. Short words in the morning make a long day.

Never let any fault that you have committed go by until you have confessed it and are forgiven.

Never forget that the nearest approach to heaven on earth is where two souls rival each other in unselfishness.

Never be contented until you know that both of you are walking in the straight and narrow road, each helping the other.

Never forget that marriage is ordained of God and that His blessing alone can make it what it ought to be.

Never let your human hopes stop short of the Home Eternal.

The wife will probably have to make more adjustments than the husband because her life is more centered in the home. She takes his name instead of her own. She changes her place of residence, not only from her parental home, but perhaps to a place far distant. She must leave the security of her former home for a new security that she and her husband must build for themselves. She has to change her role in life to the manifold duties of housekeeper, homemaker, business manager, nurse, companion, cook, and sweetheart. To do all this requires adjustment in her way of life and thought.

These are some of the adjustments one group of young wives said they had to face and make if they wanted a happy home.

> To give and to take. The idea that before you make decisions you have someone else to consider.
>
> The first thing to do is to think about church together, and remember that there are two to satisfy and not just one.
>
> Adjusting to the husband's family. Assuming full responsibility for a household. Learning to think more of the other than of myself.
>
> Sharing my toothpaste and keeping the cap on the top. Keeping my clothes closet straight.
>
> The most difficult adjustment after marriage was to have to learn that my dream angel had to eat like any other mortal and was used to the kind of food that mother cooked and not the fancy cooking I did, but we both lived through it.
>
> To adjust and control my temper and impatience. I had to learn to share instead of having everything my way.
>
> I am still making adjustments. Putting the other first was one of the hardest things I had to learn.
>
> The most difficult adjustment in early marriage was to cope with my husband's temper. He very easily flew off the handle, and I had to learn to control myself.
>
> Learning how to give as well as take and that I was wrong as often as I was right was my most difficult adjustment. Respecting my husband's views in relation to my own.
>
> Making my parents accept and treat my husband as they ought. They did well on big things, but forgot on the little things. Be completely honest and frank with each other. Don't let the faults on either side interfere with your relationships with your children. Remember your love for each other above any minor disagreements.

The man must make adjustments too. His time is no longer
his own. It must be shared with someone else. His interests
are now centered in one person and in her well-being. His
money is no longer his alone, but must be shared with another.
As a matter of fact, women today control 85 per cent of the
buying power of the nation. They buy 75 per cent of the
things that men use. The little lady who with one hand rocks
the cradle, has her other hand on the nation's finances. The
women of this country own 75 per cent of the suburban homes
and hold 60 per cent of the nation's savings. Four out of five
insurance policies are in their name. They own 40 per cent of
the real estate in America. They are the majority stockholders
in many great corporations. That is quite an adjustment for
a man to face when it relates to his own finances too.

A number of young husbands out of their experience say
these are adjustments they had to make.

> It is a much more serious step than most people realize.
> When you do realize the responsibilities, accept them and
> make good.
>
> Don't let other people tell you how to run your life. Find
> out together, but don't live with your in-laws.
>
> Be sure you are really in love, not a passing fancy or
> puppy love, but the one and only.
>
> Think before answering a harsh or pessimistic remark.
>
> Be open-minded toward the other's faults, and remember
> the faults you have yourself.
>
> Be sure that you show your love in ways that mean the
> most to your life partner as well as in the ways that mean the
> most to you.
>
> Change "I" to "we" and "us."

There are other adjustments that both must make. You must
learn the importance of the little things of life, such as tidiness,

neatness, and attractiveness; the courtesies of life, and the expression of gratitude and appreciation. You need to learn to respect each other's likes and dislikes as to food and clothes, amusements and ways of housekeeping. You will do well to recognize and understand each other's moods, to know when to speak and when to keep quiet, to recognize that there are special times of tension when one or both are tired and weary and more inclined to be irritable. You have to learn to understand, and to trust when you cannot quite understand. Always maintain respect and confidence for each other, for love dies if faith and trust disappear. You learn that each must have a certain measure of freedom within the marriage bond, freedom to grow and develop, to pursue your own interests, though always with due regard for the other. You learn to develop common interests and goals, things to talk about and do together. You learn that there are some things you have to wait for.

There are really three homes you must consider if marriage is to exceed your expectations. The first is your family home where Christ is in reality the head of the house. The second is the church home where you worship together and where you and your children grow together in faith and in Christian love and service. The third is your heavenly home, as you look toward the day when you will be separated for a time, knowing that through faith you will be together again in that house not made with hands, eternal in the heavens. To love and cherish those three homes is to find that yours will be a happiness that increases with the years and reaches out into eternity.

What such a love and understanding can mean is beautifully portrayed in the play by R. E. Sherwood entitled *There Shall Be No Night*. The scene is in Finland just after the first

Russian attack of the war. The husband, who is a doctor, tells his wife, whom he had met and married in America, that he wants her to leave him and go back to Boston. She objects and says that her place is in Finland with him. He in turn insists that she must go where she will be safe and that she must go at once. As she continues to object he says, "But only those can stay here now who are doing something essential. There will not be enough bread for all and those who are not essential must go." She replies, "Then you mean that I'm not essential. I have no place, no significance, no meaning." She finally wears him down until he admits that his deepest concern is really for her safety and security and her welfare. He goes on, "I'll be working in a laboratory and that laboratory may be wiped out and the work of the years may be gone. All I have left is you and my love for you. That's all I have." She says, "You see, I am essential. I may be just a woman, but I am essential because you love me." Through his tears and hers, he says, "Yes, yes, you are, because I love you." It is that kind of love and concern for the other that opens the door to the best of love and home for all those who are "no longer two but one."

A House with a Home Inside

ONE summer in England I visited in the home of a lovely English couple. The husband is the pastor of the famous Westham Chapel in the East End of London. All around their home and church was grim evidence of the destructiveness of war. The couple in themselves revealed the peace and assurance of a deep faith and the devotion and consecration of true love. As I stood talking with them in the doorway of their home I understood something of their spirit when I saw the motto over the entrance, "Lord, make my house Thine until Thine shall be mine." Theirs is a house with a home inside.

Quite by contrast I think of another house. It is a beautiful, modern dwelling with lovely landscaping in a fine residential section. To look at it you would think it must surely be the dwelling place of a happy family. But I have seen two unhappy couples live in that house, and I have watched both those homes break and fail. There is a house, a beautiful house, but it has had no home inside.

What makes the difference? Edgar Guest says, it does take "a heap of living in a house to make it home." It takes that and more. It takes consecration and faith, a feeling of partnership with God, and a sense of the presence of Christ.

The coming of children helps to make a house a home. It is so important that a Christian home have children if at all possible. Such is the plan of God. The average couple should have children within a year or two after marriage while they are still young. It is unwise to wait too long, though there should be time for adjustment and for necessary savings.

Children should not come between the parents nor should they take the place of a parent in the thought of either husband or wife. Rather they are a sacred trust to be cherished by husband and wife together and to be led in the paths of right and truth and life everlasting. No couple standing by the bedside of their firstborn child can ever quite get away from the wonder of it all. What a sacred privilege it is to share with God in the creating, training, and guiding of the next generation. In that hour you would be strange indeed not to thank God for the parents who gave you life and to ask God to help you be a good parent in turn. How could you do it alone? Those who take this responsibility seriously will be blessed as was the mother of John and Charles Wesley of whom someone has said, "Hers was the privilege of being a kind of pioneer electrical engineer, for out of the spark she fanned to flame in the hearts of her children there came light and radiance and power for a whole nation and a whole world."

Children bring great responsibilities but also deep and abiding joys. The verse by Edgar Guest entitled "No Children in the House" pictures the childless home:

> No children in the house to play,
> It must be hard to live that way!
> I wonder what the people do
> When night comes on and the work is through
> With no glad little folks to shout,

No eager feet to race about,
No youthful tongues to chatter on
About the joy that's been and gone;
The house may be a castle fine,
But what a lonely place to dine.

No children in the house at all,
No finger marks upon the wall,
No corner where the toys are piled,
Sure identification of a child.
No little lips to breathe the prayer
That God shall keep you in his care,
No glad caress and welcome sweet
When night returns you to your street;
No little lips a kiss to give,
Oh, what a lonely way to live.[1]

I remember seeing a painting in Munich which showed a young girl looking in a mirror. But she did not see herself. She saw rather the picture of an old woman wearing many jewels with others spread out on her dressing table. The girl was portrayed as having to choose either all these earthly riches and pleasures and later loneliness or to find the joys of children and home. There really is no choice for those who know what children can mean. "Blessed is the man whose quiver is full of them" (Psalm 127:5).

The normal couple should have children, but it is unfair to judge harshly those who do not because you might not know all the facts. There are many who seek to meet the hunger in their hearts for children either through lives of service to others or through adopting children. Some of the happiest parents I know, and some of the finest and happiest children

[1] From *Collected Verse of Edgar A. Guest*; copyright, 1934, by The Reilly & Lee Co., Chicago, and reprinted with their permission.

as well, are in homes made glad by adopting babies who needed a home. This should always be done only in consultation with your doctor and the proper legal authorities or child welfare agencies.

The number of children in the home should be determined in part by the health of the parents, the security of the home, the amount of income, and conditions of employment. Children should come by choice and not by mere chance, a choice that is made in conscious fellowship with God. Each married couple must face honestly and prayerfully the matter of planned parenthood. The wise and Christian use of such birth control measures as your doctor advises are, of course, essential if children are to be planned and provided for. You will find a serious and sincere difference between most Protestants and Catholics with reference to this matter. Birth control is a sin if it is used only to further personal pleasure or to keep children from ever coming into a home that should have them. A planned parenthood program, however, is fundamentally right and wise in its effort to provide protection for those who should not have children and guidance for those who want a family they can care for properly.

Children should have a Christian home in which to grow and develop. They should be given appreciation and affection, assurance and inspiration, a chance to count for something in the world, a sense of security, recognition for what they do, and ideals that give them something to dream of and strive for. Children in such homes grow up happy and well balanced because they know they are wanted, they have an enduring home, and parents they can respect and honor, love and obey.

The proud parents of two adopted children supplied the following verse that describes the feelings of all good parents for their children:

> My little daughter is a tearose,
> Satin to the touch, wine to the lips,
> And the same delirious perfume.
> But my little son is a June apple,
> Firm and cool and scornful of too much sweetness,
> And full of tang and flavor,
> And better than bread to the hungry.
> O wild winds and clumsy pilfering bees,
> With the whole world to be wanton in,
> Will you not spare my little tearose?
> O ruthless, blind creatures,
> Who lay eggs of evil at the core of life,
> Pass by my one red apple, so firm and sound.

Often you find father and mother competing for the affection and interest of the children or divided and at odds about their care and discipline. The result is a home of tension and unhappiness and sometimes a broken home. Children usually, however, draw a couple together as they call out the best that husband and wife can give. Each parent then realizes how important the other is.

One thing you should remember, do not try to foist your own loves and hates and prejudices on your children. Do not try to shape them into your own pattern or seek to force them to fulfill all your own unrealized dreams. Let them be themselves, the selves God meant them to be. In the book *My Son, My Son,* later made into a movie, two boys grow up with no religious training. One father has a great love for Ireland and a hatred of England and dreams of the day when he can help to free Ireland. He puts into his son all the hatred of his own heart, and the boy finally dies a miserable death

trying to measure up to his father's expectations. The other
father wants his son to have everything he wanted and never
had. So he lavishes everything on the son. The boy is so spoiled
he makes a miserable failure of life and finally the father has
to see his son pay with his life for the price of murder.

From the day children come to the home all in the family
need more than ever the strength and help of God and this
admonition, "Children, obey your parents in the Lord, for
this is right. Honor thy father and mother that it may be well
with thee and thou mayest live' long on the earth. And, ye
fathers, provoke not your children to wrath, but bring them
up in the nurture and admonition of the Lord" (Ephesians
6:1). Cora W. Riley's " 'Twas a Sheep" is an earnest prayer for
guidance:

> 'Twas a sheep not a lamb that strayed away
> In the parable Jesus told;
> A grown-up sheep that had gone astray
> From the ninety-and-nine in the fold.
>
> Out on the hillside, out in the cold,
> It was a sheep the good shepherd sought;
> Back to the flock, safe to the fold,
> It was a sheep that the shepherd brought.
>
> And why for the sheep should we earnestly long
> And earnestly hope and pray?
> Because there is danger if they go wrong,
> They will lead their lambs astray.
>
> The lambs will follow the sheep, you know,
> Wherever the sheep may stray,
> When the sheep go wrong it will not be long
> 'Til the lambs are as wrong as they.

So with the sheep we earnestly plead
For the sake of the lambs today;
If the sheep are lost, what a terrible cost
Some lambs will have to pay.

What then should parents do as children grow older? Should a tight rein be kept on them or should parents keep hands off and let them stumble? Perhaps that is one price that parental love must pay, to let children sometimes go their own way, make some mistakes and pay the price, even though they cannot pay it all. You can trust them, though, if you have given them the knowledge that God's help is real and that He will guide and strengthen them in temptation and lead them to the best use of life. You can trust them if you have taught them of Christ and lead them to faith in him as Saviour and Lord. That is part of your privilege and responsibility.

Children, too, have a responsibility in the home. "Honor thy father and thy mother," the father and mother who gave you the gift of life. Just what are you giving back to your parents? You will never know how much they loved you, how much they sacrificed for you, how much they cherished and watched over you and wished for your happiness until you are a parent yourself. Jesus is right in emphasizing the old commandment, "Honor thy father and thy mother." Honor them by the way you treat them and by the way you live before others. There is a painting that shows a mother sitting by the bed of her sick child. On her tired face is a look of concern. In her hand is her open Bible. She reads the Word seeking strength and assurance as she holds the hand of the little one who is sick. Somebody did that for you, trusted in God and did the best she could. A father labored through the years to give you your chance in life. "Honor thy father and thy mother." As you do you will find it adds much to the joy of the home of your dreams.

Treat each child as an individual. Inspire and encourage each to make his own contribution to the world and your life will be all the richer for it. One Christian homemaker whose five children are all outstanding Christians and public servants found this was true in her life. She says, "When I was a young lady I felt it would be the highest calling and greatest honor to be called of God to do full-time work on some mission field. The conviction came that God wanted me to serve him as a homemaker. I became increasingly happy when I realized that my field of service could be multiplied five times through our children. With God as my partner and daily guide, it was a joyful experience, striving to be a helpful companion to my husband and to instill into our children the importance of 'seeking first the Kingdom of God.' I cannot think of any work where God's wisdom is more needed than that of building a Christian home. For any measure of success, I humbly express gratitude to my Heavenly Father."

> Coward and wayward and weak,
> I change with the changing sky,
> Today so eager and brave,
> Tomorrow not willing to try;
> But He never gives in,
> So we two shall win—Jesus and I.

Plan new and interesting things to do as individuals and as a family. Beware of doing for your children things they can and should learn to do for themselves. Teach them early the importance of personal responsibility and dependability, seeking increasingly to develop their independence rather than stressing or encouraging their dependence on you. Remember we learn something from the experience of others, but much of what we learn comes the hard way from costly personal experience. You profited from mistakes and hard knocks and so will they.

Remember your own shortcomings and temper justice with love and mercy. Let your discipline always be fair, firm, and consistent, always administered in love rather than because you are hurt or angry. Try always to remember how things seem to a child and that they do not view life with your adult perspective and viewpoint. The older you grow the harder this may be, but it is all the more important. This is also a reason for having your children while you are young enough to share life and activities with them and understand and appreciate their point of view. Let the children share increasingly in making the family plans and decisions rather than trying to rule them with unbending authority and by decrees for which they can see no reason and get no explanation.

Be sure your children know always that you love and trust them and expect the best from them, regardless of what others may say or do. Let them understand that they and their friends are always welcome in the home. Let it be the center of their life and thought, but remember that the older they get the more you must be willing to trust them and let them go.

Stimulate in your children a love of the good and beautiful in every area of life and help them to live as world citizens. Encourage them to respect and love all races and creeds and nations, and beware of passing on to them old and outworn prejudices and taboos. Help each one to get the training and find the place of usefulness in life for which under God he is best fitted.

Lead each child to a personal faith in God and Christ, membership in the church, and service with others for the good of the community and the advancement of the Kingdom of God. Teach them habits of worship and prayer and go with them to Sunday School and church. Jesus said, "Suffer the little children to come unto me and forbid them not." It is a terrible mistake to shut God out of the lives of children. As they grow older you will find how much a common religious experience helps you face the problem of combining discipline with freedom and all the other puzzles that plague the parents of today.

Do you remember the story of the boy who on Sunday morning was told by his mother as he started off to Sunday School and church, "Well, go say good-by to your father and then hurry along. You'll be late." The boy found his father reading the Sunday paper and said, "Dad, before I go I'd like to ask you one question." "What's that, son?" "How old will I have to be before I can stay home on Sunday as you do?" Quickly the father replied, "Son, you wait a minute; I'm going with you." He was a wise father, for a Christian home and a Christian church home working together can produce the kind of children the world needs.

Is your home all that it might be? Whether you live in a mansion or a cottage, on a farm or in the city, in an apartment or a trailer, it is the spirit within that makes the difference. I think often of a little cottage in the mountains where my father and mother and the children and grandchildren would gather in the summer. At the close of the day as we sat around the fire my father would take the Bible and read to us. On his knees he would pray for his home, for the homes of his children, for our church homes, and the work we were called of God to do in the world. He would lift us up in his prayers until we caught a glimpse of God and the heavenly home.

"In my father's house are many mansions," Jesus said. "If it were not so I would have told you." By the miracle of God's grace and love we all can have homes in this life that are happy and enduring and a heavenly home, "a house not made with hands, eternal in the heavens." One can never quite get away from such a heritage of faith, such a noble concept of life and home, here and hereafter. The poem "So Long As There Are Homes" by Grace Noll Crowell pictures the "house with a home inside":

> So long as there are homes to which men turn
> > At close of day;
> So long as there are homes where children are,
> > Where women stay;
> If love and loyalty and faith be found
> > Across these sills,
> A stricken nation can recover from
> > Its gravest ills.
>
> So long as there are homes where fires burn
> > And there is bread;
> So long as there are homes where lamps are lit
> > And prayers are said;
> Although a people falter through the dark
> > And nations grope,
> With God himself back of these little homes
> > We have sure hope.[2]

[2] From *Light of the Years* by Grace Noll Crowell. Copyright, 1936, by Harper & Brothers and reprinted with permission.

Chapter

IX

Headaches and Heartaches in Marriage

A COUPLE who have been happily married sixty years give as their prescription for happiness in marriage their version of the golden rule, "Do unto one another as you would a month before marriage." Of course, that is not enough, but it is a help. Just remember what you once did and what you once were and then be sure that any change in you has been for better and not for worse. You know you marry for better or for worse, but some may feel like the man in court who said, "But, Judge, she is worse than I took her for."

Many couples could profit from a simple application of the golden rule and the counsel of Paul in his letter to the Ephesians, "Let all bitterness and wrath and anger and clamour and evil speaking be put away from you with all malice; and be ye kind one to another, tenderhearted, forgiving one another even as God for Christ's sake hath forgiven you" (Ephesians 4:31).

Many a husband who takes pride in being a good provider and many a wife whose immaculate house is her pride and joy could profit from the lesson in this little verse:

Curtains fresh and snowy-crisp,
Hearthstone swept of every wisp,
Mirror-like each pan and pot,
Muffins tender, steaming hot,
Floors immaculate and shining;
Voice irascible or whining,
Puckered brow and fretful lips,
Eyes that witness joy's eclipse,
Color-blind to all but gray—
Pity that she can't one day
Leave untidy some top shelf
While she renovates herself!

Most marriages can and do succeed. As a matter of fact, almost any marriage can succeed if both parties want it to and if each is willing to do his part. Both must be ready to take the help of God and the church and to profit from the experience of others.

The law of averages is on your side. Statistics show not only that most people marry but also that most marriages are successful, though far too many fail. In 1950, for example, 1,669,-934[1] couples were married. Half of the men in the United States are married before they are twenty-four and half the girls are married before they are twenty-two. Three fourths of our population are married before they reach thirty years of age. Contrast that with Ireland where at the age of thirty only one third of the men and half of the girls are married.

At the same time the divorce rate is declining. In 1950 there were 386,000 divorces in this country, a decrease of 2 per cent from 1949 and 39 per cent below the record total in 1946 when 613,000 marriages were legally dissolved. Many of those were

---

[1] Taken from *The World Almanac*.

a natural result of the war, either hasty marriages that had to be dissolved, or marriages that separation had broken, as is evidenced by the fact that there were only 450,000 divorces in 1947. More alarming, however, is the fact that in 1946 there were 7,450,000 homes in this country where the husband was absent and 300,000 homes where the mother was gone, not because of death, but by separation.

This is bad to be sure, but the situation has improved greatly in the years since World War II. For a true picture do not overlook the fact that in that same year there were 35,000,000 united and going homes in America. The picture is not all dark. Your home can succeed. Of course, many of those 35,000,000 homes are not as happy as they might be. Someone has estimated that one third of them are fairly happy, another third are just about getting along, and the other third have really found the heaven-on-earth that marriage can bring and that our Christian faith can help many of the others to enjoy.

A pastor went to visit a home where the people were not Christian. When the door was opened he said, "Peace be to this house." The man of the house looked at him grimly and said, "There's no peace in this house," and slammed the door. The preacher very quietly went his way. In a few days the husband called him and said, "I'm sorry I was so rude. Won't you come and see us?" The preacher went gladly and told them about Jesus Christ and the difference he could make in their lives and in their home. He led them to faith in Christ and soon they joined the church. Later the husband said to him, "I'll never forget how I slammed the door in your face. There hadn't been any peace in our house for twenty-three years, but there is such a difference now."

O blessed house, that cheerfully receiveth
Thy visits, Jesus Christ, the soul's true Friend;
That, far beyond all other guests, believeth
It must to Thee its warmest cheer extend;
Where every heart to Thee is fondly turning,
Where every eye for Thee with pleasure speaks,
Where all to know Thy will are truly yearning,
And every one to do it promptly seeks.

O blessed house, where man and wife, united
In Thy true love, hath both one heart and mind;
Where both to Thy salvation are invited,
And in Thy doctrine both contentment find;
Where both, to Thee, in truth, forever cleaving
In Joy, in grief, make Thee their only stay,
And fondly hope in Thee to be believing,
Both in the good and in the evil day.

Every marriage faces good and evil days. Wise are those who prepare for the hard days while they enjoy the good and who build a comradeship that is adequate for either. A woman who has helped many with their problems tells of her own testing. During a depression she and her husband had to leave a luxurious apartment for a simple home with few conveniences. As they sat together the first night in their new home, seemingly so poor and inadequate as compared with all they had enjoyed before, she turned to him rather overwhelmed by it all and said with a sigh, "Well, we're *here*." He turned with a smile, put his hand in hers and said, "My dear, the important thing is *we're* here." She tells now with a smile how his understanding and their common love and devotion did bring good out of what had seemed at the time to be an evil day.

Some heartaches root in the inevitable crises of life. It may be financial difficulties, or a great decision, or a move to another place and separation from friends or loved ones, illness, or the death of one who is near and dear. I remember a painting in the Louvre in Paris that pictured a humble French cottage. The young wife has died and the young husband and his father are broken at the loss of the one who was love and life and light to her husband and their home. In such hours it is good to know that "God is our refuge and strength, a very present help in trouble" (Psalm 127:1).

Marriages are often wrecked by such character failures as dishonesty, untruthfulness, cheating, and lying. Gambling takes a heavy toll, and the use of alcohol ruins many homes. There is much of wisdom in the warning in Ephesians, "Be not drunk with much wine, a thing in which excess is so easy" (5:18). Did you know that three out of every one hundred employed people in this country are alcoholics? Those alcoholics lose on the average of twenty-two days of work a year. The wages lost by alcoholics in one year run up over four hundred million dollars. I have never heard of an alcoholic who started out deliberately to be one. Recent studies show that 55 per cent of America's alcoholics started as social drinkers and 45 per cent were caused by personality problems.

Many a wife comes to me disturbed about her marriage and what liquor is doing to it. I ask, "Did your husband drink when you married him?" "Oh, yes," is often the reply, "but I didn't think it would be as bad as it is."

In many cases it does get progressively worse and the whole family suffers. I think of one wife who called to say, "Can't you help me stop drinking?" It had already cost her the love of her husband and now she was rapidly losing the respect of her children and she faced the future with dread unless someone could help. Nor can I forget the husband who came saying, "For God's sake, help me to stop drinking. I'll lose my wife, my family, my business, and everything." Think well about the risks you take before you marry one who drinks, especially if there is any record of drunkenness or chronic alcoholism.

It certainly is a mistake to expect that marriage will automatically solve all your problems, or to think that just because you are married all your problems are over. You will probably find a good many more. It is foolish to think that marriage is going to be just a continuing romantic experience, though the spirit of courtship and romance ought to go on. The fact is that the scene will shift quickly from "Moonlight and Roses" to "Daylight and Dishes."

No marriage is going to succeed without work. If yours is to be all that it ought to be you must enter it not only with an expectation of success but with a willingness to work to that end. To do that will call out the very best that is in you. Many marriages break up in the first year or two just because of a failure at this point. One or both are disappointed or disillusioned because they expected the wrong things or because of an unwillingness to do the work that is necessary.

Other marriages fail after a longer period of trial because the whole marriage relationship has just deteriorated. The two are unwilling or unable to make the necessary adjustments and to build up common interests. Little by little barriers grow up between them. Often this process of separation and deterioration is so slow that the couple do not realize the seriousness of the situation until some crisis reveals how far apart they are and how little they have in common.

They say a wife and husband, bit by bit,
Can rear between themselves a mighty wall,
So thick they cannot speak with ease through it,
Nor can they see across, it stands so tall.
Its nearness frightens them, but each alone
Is powerless to tear its bulk away,
And each, dejected, wishes he had known
For such a wall, some magic thing to say.

So let us build with master art, my dear,
A bridge of love between your life and mine,
A bridge of tenderness, and very near,
A bridge of understanding, strong and fine,
Till we have formed so many lovely ties,
There never will be room for walls to rise.

Some marriages do fail because of seemingly little, though very important things that cause tension, such as neglecting the courtesies of life, forgetting anniversaries and birthdays, or the habit of saying harsh and cruel things when one is tired or tense. Billy Sunday once said, "If you want your wife to be an angel, don't treat her like the devil," and he was about right.

Learn, for example, in planning your finances to make allowances for certain irrational expenditures. The wife is going to feel she must have a new hat or a "precious antique" once in a while no matter how many bills are unpaid, and the husband is going to buy a new golf stick or some new gadget that catches his masculine fancy. Both will make foolish purchases and mistakes and each must understand and make allowances for it. If the husband spends too much on a birthday or anniversary gift, the wife should be thankful he did not forget it rather than make too great a fuss at the time about the amount of money involved. A little later the gift can be exchanged if necessary, or a moral pointed out, but not just at the moment.

Another threat to successful marriage is summed up in a word that covers a multitude of sins. We call it incompatibility. Evidence of this difficulty is usually apparent before marriage to those with eyes to see. It is fatal if either one is unwilling to adjust his way of life to the desires of the other or if one tries always to dominate the other. Only as you have a sense of humor and a willingness to adjust will you really solve this problem of incompatibility. Let me illustrate it in two verses. "Why Is Man the Master?" was written by Ann Rogers, a young wife who has learned the secret for herself. "When Mother Thinks We Ought to Go" was written by Edgar Guest. One speaks for the women; the other for the men. The woman says:

> Why is man the master?
> Why is he the king?
> Why is he superior
> In almost everything?

> Why do men get angry
> And say nagging isn't nice,
> Yet when they do the selfsame thing
> They think it's good advice?

> And when a woman questions
> She's too curious, she'll find;
> But the same impulse within the male
> Shows a scientific mind.

> A woman's private life should be
> An open book, you see.
> Then why should every type of man
> Insist his should be free?

And when a man is masterly
Women say, "We all abhor it."
But secretly, within our hearts,
We find that we adore it.

The man puts it this way:

When Mother thinks we ought to go
To see a moving picture show,
Though I've a book I'd like to read
I put the volume down with speed.

When Mother says, "We ought to do
Your old arm chair in navy blue,"
Though I am rather fond of red
I promptly vote for blue, instead.

When Mother looks across at me
And says, "My dear, take no more tea!"
Though much I'd like a second cup
I promptly give the notion up.

When I've rebelled as now and then
I have, like all the stubborn men,
And let my will run free and strong,
My judgment usually was wrong.

Now for the second piece of pie
I've ceased to ask when Mother's nigh,
And reconciled to growing old,
I've learned to do just as I'm told.[2]

Such problems and tensions can bring headaches and heartaches or, if faced with love and good humor and common sense, they can help build up happy memories of heart-warming experiences that can be a blessing through the years. If you want

[2] Copyright, 1933, by Edgar A. Guest. Reprinted with permission of The Reilly & Lee Co., Chicago.

your marriage to succeed, cultivate such attitudes between you and keep the spirit of Christ in your own life. His spirit and presence can save your love and your home. As you trust in Him to bring you safely through the difficult hours of life, make this old hymn the prayer of your heart:

> Jesus, Saviour, pilot me
> Over life's tempestuous sea;
> Unknown waves before me roll,
> Hiding rock and treacherous shoal;
> Chart and compass come from thee;
> Jesus, Saviour, pilot me.

Chapter

X

Broken Hearts and Broken Homes

IN A single year, recently, twice as many homes in the United States were broken by separation and divorce as were broken by death. This tragic fact reveals the enormity of our problem and the importance of helping all who marry to find the joy of true love and lasting family ties.

Since the children are usually the ones who pay the greater price in separation and divorce, think of them before you give up. You brought them into the world. Society is concerned, too, that our homes should succeed. A great percentage of our delinquent children and the problem cases in our courts come from broken homes. A leading criminologist says that the principal environmental causes of crime are improper parental guidance and broken homes.

Experience indicates that the average divorce rate for couples who are active together in the same church home is only about 2 per cent, far less than the rate among those who are not active in any church. Check this in your own experience. How many cases of separation or divorce do you know where both parties were active in the same church? Probably very few, if any. A common church home helps husband and wife to be Christian in all of life's relationships and provides many bonds of faith, fellowship, and service to hold them together.

Dr. Norman Vincent Peale tells of a young wife who came to him in distress, her marriage a failure, her home about to break up. He knew that they had let Christian faith and worship slowly slip out of their lives. He suggested that she and her husband pray about it that night, and she promised to try. That evening she reminded her husband that when they were first married they had prayed together regularly but had long neglected it. Touched by the memory, they knelt and prayed together for the first time in months. As they prayed, barriers were broken down and they found love and God again and a home was saved.

Many a marriage could be saved and any home will be blessed by the spirit of such a prayer as this by James Dillet Freeman entitled "Lord, Bless This Home":

> Lord, bless this house and bless us all
> In care and pleasure, great or small;
> Blest be the door friends enter by
> And windows that let in the sky
> And roof above and walls about
> That shut the world and weather out!
> Lord, make my house a mansion of
> Abiding loveliness and love,
> A friendly, comfortable place.
> Let pleasant talk like firelight grace
> These rooms, and may friends linger long
> To join in laughter or a song.
> Blest be these rooms for work or play!
> Oh, let my house be sometimes gay
> And sometimes still as candlelight.
> Be with us, Lord, both day and night;
> Blest be our labor and our rest;

Our waking and our sleep be blest.
In care and pleasure, great or small,
Lord, bless this house and bless us all!

Dr. T. H. Van de Velde in his monumental book entitled *Ideal Marriage* says truly, "Two lovers promise the highest, loveliest, hardest task a man or woman can undertake, to control the current of emotions and direct it always toward each other." Surely in such a task we need, and can have, the help of the God of love. He goes on, "The true marriage is not one without conflicts, but the one that is ever reconciling its conflicts."

One wife whose husband was untrue and failed her terribly went with him to talk with their minister about their future. The husband had repented deeply and sincerely, and she was willing to try again to rebuild their home. After a frank discussion of their problems and a word of prayer together she said, "If you have faith in God and in each other you can build over again."

A number of factors have contributed to marital instability and the increasing number of broken homes. Two judges in an Eastern city recently were asked to give the chief reasons for the divorces in their courts. One said, "I blame primarily the lack of religion. Where there is no religion there is no civic or social responsibility. Where there is no social responsibility there is no family responsibility and lacking that, everything goes out the window." The other judge said, "Overindulgence in alcoholic beverages is the cause of disagreement in the large percentage of cases that come before my court."

The great increase in the number of women working outside the home has contributed substantially to our increasing divorce rate. Womanhood offers no greater privilege than that of building a home and rearing a family. Yet there are now many other fields open to women and many prefer them to an unhappy or insecure marriage. A wife who is dissatisfied with her life with her husband does not have to stay with him for support. Often she can do better financially alone.

There has also been a change in the historic functions of the family. Home was once the place where children received much of their education. Recreation largely centered in the home. Today radio and television are helping to keep it there and many homes are the stronger for it. The home was once a place of protection. Every man's house was his own castle and he felt called upon to keep his guns handy for defense against his enemies. Now recreation and education and these protective functions are all carried on largely through people or institutions outside the family unit.

There was a time when many things were produced in the home both for use and for sale. Children were a financial asset rather than a liability. The home was once the center of a great deal of industry and production which is now carried on outside the home and again, except in rural areas, the home has lost a function that once helped to keep the family together.

This change in function is also evident in religion. The father was once the priest and religious instruction was largely centered in the home. Now some fathers have as much trouble helping junior with his Sunday School homework as with his algebra because father just does not know about the spiritual growth of his child. Bible reading and prayer have vanished from many a fireside. Little by little we are trying to draw the home and church and school into a closer relationship so that the home can again be an effective center of religious life and thought. Only as we strengthen the spiritual foundations and functions of the home can we hope to decrease the number of broken homes and broken hearts.

The transient population of this country has a great deal to do with the increasing divorce rate. In our cities many marry who are comparative strangers. They marry into families about whose background they know little or nothing. It amazes me how many couples think seriously of getting married when the girl has never seen his people and he has never seen hers. They really know about each other only what that one individual has told them. This was at the root of many of the marriage failures during the war. Strangers married strangers from unknown families. There was a time when most young people married in the community in which they grew up, and the couple and their families had known each other through the years. Conditions differ greatly now and all of these factors have helped in the trend toward increasing tension and unhappiness in marriage.

One evening in my study I had two appointments. The first was with a young couple who came to be married. I had talked with them previously at some length and felt certain they were ready for marriage. We signed all the papers and went into the chapel where I pronounced them husband and wife in a simple, quiet service, and they went on their way rejoicing.

A little later for my second appointment there came, first a woman and then a man. They did not come together. Just a few short years before they too had stood in that same chapel and taken those same vows. They too had left the chapel with the same high hopes and dreams. Now they came back separately and stared into each other's eyes. First one and then the other poured out a story of bitterness and accusation that would make one's blood run cold. One of them had asked that we talk together in the faint hope that there might be a reconciliation. The other had already filed for a divorce. That night I had to see a couple I had married face the fact that their marriage was at an end. They went their separate ways, and I saw a marriage die. One cannot share in a sorrow and heartbreak like that without realizing how important it is that those who want to stay married start right and stay right.

It is a sad fact in American life that in the past ten years eight million persons have been divorced. If the present trend continues this year nearly eight hundred thousand more Americans will go through the divorce courts. Two fifths of the couples involved will have minor-age children, and three hundred thousand children will be involved in the divorce actions. This means that well over a million people this year will have the heartbreak, the tragedy, and the problems that arise out of divorce in addition to all of those who were divorced in previous years and are still faced with the problems divorce can bring.

If the present trend continues within the next five years some three fourths of that eight hundred thousand people will have tried marriage again and only half of them will have found the happiness they seek.

Is divorce ever right? It is never good. It is never easy. It sometimes is right. Divorce occasionally is the best way out of a serious difficulty or dilemma. There is always heartache connected with it. The children usually pay the greater price though the parents pay a price too. Many who have been divorced, thinking it a good way out of their troubles, wish later they had tried harder and longer to succeed in marriage before giving up.

An older man some years ago came to his pastor and said, "Will you please talk to my sister?" It developed that she had left her husband, moved into her brother's home and sued for divorce. As the minister talked with her the brother came in and said to his sister, "I want you to know something. I never want you to have the unhappiness I have known in the years since my divorce. You don't know how unhappy I have been. You are welcome to stay here as long as you wish, but for the happiness you may know, go back and try again, for when a man and woman are married and divorced they are never quite the same again."

Consider carefully the cost in loneliness, in social difficulties, in church disapproval, and in the loss of financial security, either because of the lack of income or because you have to pay alimony. Be sure you are right before you go ahead.

In one of his best stories O. Henry tells of a couple who thought their marriage was a failure. Husband and wife each begin to pack their things to leave. The wife wonders who should have the baby's shoes, the shoes of a child that died as an infant and left them childless. Thinking the husband might want them, she puts them on his table and leaves the room. When he comes in and finds the baby's shoes, many memories are awakened and a few moments later husband and wife are crying in each other's arms, holding the baby's shoes between them. The memories and the tears helped to wash away the differences that had clouded their life together and they were one again.

However, it may well be that after consulting with pastors, lawyers or marriage counselors you decide that the best thing to do is to end your marriage, tragic though divorce may be. In any such settlement, however, put your children's welfare first, even before your own. Sometimes divorce is better for the children. They ought not to have to face the day-after-day hostility of two parents, though it is just as tragic sometimes after a divorce for children to be tossed back and forth, a few months here and a few months there, between parents who are constantly trying to paint a black, unfavorable picture of each other.

If you are divorced, you may have to face the question, Is it ever right to marry again? Sometimes it is, if it accords with the spirit of Christ and will give the two and perhaps some children a truly Christian home. If you feel that remarriage is the answer in your case, take time enough to be sure that the things that caused your former unhappiness will not be present again. The chances are that you, yourself, are more mature. You know more what to expect and what not to expect. Take enough time to be sure that this new home is "founded upon a rock."

Even though you may come through every other trial and make all the adjustments called for by life together, some day the home will be broken. Death will come, as it must to us all, and your heart will be heavy as one goes on to the eternal home. You cannot know the joys of love nor have the satisfaction of being together without also facing the pain of parting. Homes will be broken and hearts, too, by "the last enemy, death." Whittier tells of the sadness of one

> Who has not learned in hours of faith
> The truth to flesh and sense unknown,
> That life is ever Lord of death,
> And love can never lose its own.

If we are linked by faith with God in Christ, life goes on and love is not defeated. In the face of death, how triumphant the Christian can be. Did not Jesus say, "Peace I leave with you, my peace I give unto you. Not as the world giveth, give I unto you. Let not your heart be troubled, neither let it be afraid. I go to prepare a place for you" (John 14:27).

When you are united in faith in Him who made that promise not even death can separate you forever. Though you will eventually be separated for a time by death, you will be together again in the eternal home with the one you have loved and lost a while. Some years ago my own mother passed away after a serious operation. My father had gone on ahead a number of years before. She had kept his picture with her most treasured belongings, and had kept him in spirit close to her heart. The day she was going to the operating room for an operation from which she never even regained consciousness, she said to my brother, "Good-by, Buddy, I have a date with a handsomer man." Within twenty-four hours she was with him, with the one she had loved and cherished through the years, together again in their eternal home. Yes, those whom God hath joined together will never be put asunder.

> O Holy Saviour, friend unseen,
> Since on thine arm thou bidst me lean;
> Help me throughout life's varying scene,
> By faith to cling to thee.
> Though faith and hope may long be tried
> I ask not, need not, ought beside;
> How safe, how calm, how satisfied,
> The souls that cling to thee.

Such, then, is our faith. As we seek to build beautiful and enduring homes, and as we strive to be worthy of love and its joys and privileges, we can have the help of Christ in it all. He can give us life and love that the world cannot defeat and death cannot end, a bond that will remain unbroken for time and for eternity.

XI

The Lonely Years

FACING life alone will be a problem for some who marry late or who never marry, and for others who lose their loved one by death or separation. How can you face life's lonely hours or years as so many others do—bravely, triumphantly, and beautifully?

We occasionally laugh at "old maids" or "old bachelors." Yet if we stop to think, most of us have reason to give thanks for some unmarried or bereaved relative or friend who has been a blessing to us and to others. Though some of the greatest joys of life may have been denied them, still other paths opened that brought them genuine happiness and satisfaction. Someone has wisely said, "If you cannot give yourself to one, give yourself in service to many. Do for them what you would want someone to do for you."

You can "live alone and like it." One good woman who has done it beautifully through the years says, "Yes, but you don't have to face life alone." She and others have learned the secret not only of making friends and finding channels of usefulness in life but also the secret Jesus knew when he said to his disciples, "I am not alone; the Father is with me." A sense of companionship and comradeship with the Almighty is at the heart of any adequate solution of the problems of loneliness. Jesus' life set him apart from others. He never married. He faced most of the problems that confront others who live alone and yet at the close of his earthly life he was able to say, "In the world you will have tribulation, but be of good cheer, I have overcome the world." He had no home and "no place to lay his head." Yet the ideals of love and home we cherish are ours largely because of him. We have a Lord who understands all of life, our joys and sorrows, our happiness and our heartaches. Samuel Longfellow knew this when he wrote the poem, "I Look to Thee":

> I look to Thee in every need,
> And never look in vain.
> I feel Thy strong and tender love,
> And all is well again;
> The thought of Thee is mightier far
> Than sin and pain and sorrow are.
>
> Discouraged in the work of life,
> Disheartened by its load,
> Shamed by its failures or its fears,
> I sink beside the road;
> But let me only think of Thee,
> And then new heart springs up in me.
>
> Thy calmness bends serene above,
> My restlessness to still,
> Around me flows Thy quickening life
> To nerve my faltering will;
> Thy presence fills my solitude,
> Thy providence turns all to good.

Embosomed deep in Thy great love,
Held in Thy law, I stand;
Thy hand, in all things I behold,
And all things in Thy hand;
Thou leadest me by unsought ways
And turn'st my mourning into praise.

With that background let us think of some of the special problems of those who face life alone as far as human companionship is concerned.

What if you have not yet found the love of your dreams or you have loved and lost and there is a hurt in your heart? As Jesus would say, "Be of good cheer." There will be more chances yet. Six girls out of seven do marry eventually, as do from 85 to 90 per cent of the men. In a government report on the marital status of persons fourteen years and over in the United States in 1951, 24.3 per cent of male persons were single; 69.9 per cent married; 4.2 per cent widowed; and 1.6 per cent divorced. Among the females, 19.1 per cent were single; 66.5 per cent married; 12.3 per cent widowed; and 2.1 per cent divorced.

Meanwhile, why not check yourself to see just what you lack and what you might do to make yourself more attractive to others. Do not just give way to a feeling of inferiority and say, "There must be something terribly wrong with me," or get so depressed about it that you make yourself less attractive. Do not inflict your troubles on those who are happily married and spoil their joy just because misery loves company. Above all else do not marry just for spite or to save your pride. Marriage without love holds little prospect for joy.

There are those, of course, who will never marry either through choice or through necessity. Let us look at the reasons why they will not marry and the attitudes that will help all who sooner or later must face life alone.

Some choose a career instead of marriage and are happy in it. Modern life has opened up a large number of opportunities for women and many have chosen to follow some career that offers independence, advancement, recognition, and an opportunity for service. They will give up joys that only marriage could bring but do so gladly because of some God-given ability or opportunity fitting them to a particular career. Others feel a call to special missionary service and gladly serve at home and abroad for Christ's sake.

Some never marry because the right person never appeared, or appeared too late, or married someone else. After a grievous disappointment some make the mistake of a hasty marriage in desperation rather than to admit defeat or to avoid facing life alone. It is folly to marry on the rebound from an unhappy experience, or just to get even with someone else, or to show that you can get married too. Such marriages usually end in disappointment. Older people often marry without a romantic experience but with the expectation that an understanding love will grow, as indeed sometimes it does. As a rule, however, it is much better not to marry unless you are sure before the wedding that you have the deep and moving love for each other that is essential for happy marriage.

Others never marry because they have responsibilities to father or mother or to younger children in the family. Certainly we honor those who make a sacrifice, often of a possible marriage, in order to meet such obligations. At the same time, we must deplore the attitude of some parents who selfishly expect that kind of sacrifice and deprive daughters or sons of the privilege of marriage so that they can be cared for or can have their own way and rule their children's lives.

Sometimes illness or a physical defect leads an individual to forego marriage. Often those who have defects can and do marry because there is enough love to compensate and a happy marriage is possible. In one very happy home the wife was confined to a wheel chair and the husband was stone deaf, but they had a successful marriage and gave the world a lovely family and an example of a genuine Christian home. It takes, however, a very real and abiding love and the willingness to sacrifice and make adjustments to build a successful home in the face of such physical handicaps.

There are some who never marry because they are not attractive personally. Often a wise and friendly counselor can be of help here. There are girls who have never really learned how to dress or to make themselves attractive. On the other hand, there are girls who are too anxious and who drive the men away. Some men, too, get so used to single life or so wrapped up in themselves that they are unwilling to make the sacrifice a home and family entail and as a consequence pay the price of loneliness in old age.

Also, individuals do not marry because they have distorted ideas about marriage or because of some emotional difficulty. This may be the result of an unfortunate experience in childhood, or an unhappy home life, or a bitter experience that has warped the whole concept of marriage. Good books, wise pastors and doctors, and trained marriage counselors can help straighten out such thinking and make a happy marriage both possible and desirable, but some will never take that help and will choose to face life alone.

In any case beware of self-pity in the lonely years. Feeling sorry for yourself is one of the most devastating attitudes in life. Guard against all this by thinking about other people. *Mrs. Wiggs in the Cabbage Patch* gives this wholesome advice, "Don't go and git sorry for yerself. That's one thing I can't stand in nobody. There's always lots of other folks yer kin be sorry fer, stid of yourself. Ain't yer proud yer ain't got a hare-lip? Why that one thought is enough to keep me from ever gittin' sorry for myself." Try the counsel of the old hymn, "Count your many blessings, name them one by one, and it will surprise you what the Lord has done."

The temptation to sexual indulgence must be met and can be conquered. Only bitterness and anguish and self-reproach can come from sin. This is true not only in cases of personal impurity but also with those who for their own self-satisfaction get involved with persons who are already married, breaking up a home and ruining three lives or more. Keep clear of such entanglements. You hurt others and you hurt yourself. Temptation is real and the desire for love is strong, but the Lord Christ can strengthen you and lead you aright. Perhaps you have already failed and you have yielded to sin and temptation. The same Lord can forgive and show you the way to purity and happiness. Stay away from temptation, break up the alliances that lead you to evil, give the Lord Christ a chance and your better self will win.

If you face life alone, you must learn to face it unselfishly if you want to be happy. That is the solution in a large measure to sex problems and others as well. Most women want children, most men want to be fathers. Most of us want and long for companionship. Sublimate that instinct and direct it into channels of love and service. It may be in helping the children of relatives, or in the church where you will have an opportunity to teach in the Sunday School and train boys and girls, or with the Boy Scouts or Girl Scouts.

Profit from the experience of one who though she faced life alone, was never really alone. She settled in a college town to make a home for two nieces and her little home became for them and for countless others a home away from home. Hers was an unforgettable life because she chose to be part of that happy and glorious company who in the spirit of Christ overcome the world by giving themselves in loving and sacrificial service for others. She knew the truth in the following lines from "My World" by Chauncey R. Piety:

> God gave my world to me,
> And I rebelliously
> Exclaimed, "How small!
> And is this all?"
> His words were sad, yet mild,
> "All that you love, my child."
>
> My self that moment died,
> And born anew I cried,
> "Love take control
> And lead my soul
> To serve my small estate!"
> And lo, my world is great![1]

Others face life alone when their homes are broken by separation or divorce. We have already dealt with some of the problems divorce brings, but it is well to stress again the importance of putting the interests of the children first, if there are children involved. Do not run the other partner down to the children. He is still daddy, and she is still mother even though you no longer live as husband and wife. Seek to develop

[1] Reprinted with permission of Chauncey R. Piety.

a wholesome life for the children in their new relationship. Their interests must also be considered if remarriage is contemplated. Many ministers and churches do not countenance such a remarriage. Others know of cases where there had been an early and unfortunate marriage, but after divorce true love did come and a second marriage and a real Christian home has been built. It can be done if there is true affection and if both are honestly willing to face the fact that the fault was not all on one side, but, looking at themselves, are resolved to be better and do better.

In any case, beware of bitterness. There will be many problems to face and many aches of mind and heart. Find for yourself the comfort and inspiration and help that prayer can bring. We do often forfeit peace and bear needless pain because we do not carry everything to God in prayer. Here is a good prayer for those who are disappointed either in life or in love:

> Oh Lord, keep me from bitterness. It is so easy
> To nurse sharp, bitter thoughts each dull, dark hour.
> Against self-pity, Man of Sorrows, defend me
> With Thy deep sweetness and Thy gentle power.
> And out of this hurt of pain and heartbreak
> Help me to harvest a new sympathy
> For suffering humankind, a wiser pity
> For those who lift a heavier cross with Thee!

It is true that out of pain and anguish can come men and women tried as by fire, finer in spirit and better able to be a blessing to others in the distressing hours of life. Trials can make us better or they can make us bitter. You choose for yourself what your spirit is to be, and, having chosen that, you have chosen what life is to mean. In the spirit of Jesus learn to say, "I am not alone; the Father is with me. In the world I have tribulation, but I shall be of good cheer, I can overcome the world."

Some day every earthly home will be broken by death. Death is but part of life and sooner or later all must face it. Sometimes it is a release, but it is always hard. How are we to get ready? First, we must live so that we will have no regrets. One of the saddest stories in all literature tells of the death of a minister's wife. After a time the minister is transferred, but before he leaves friends find him out in the little cemetery lying on the grave of his wife, sobbing and talking as though to her. The cry of his heart is, "Oh, my dear, I wasn't kind enough to you. I neglected you. I wasn't good enough to you. I see it now. Will you forgive me?" So live that there will be no such regrets, but that rather there will be stored up memories that will bless you through all the lonely years.

Unless you are willing to face the loss of your loved one by death, do not marry at all. The day must come when one of you will leave the other behind. Then, rather than blaming God for your loneliness, ought you not to thank Him for all the blessings that love and life together have brought you through the years? When death comes and with it separation, be a Christian. Accept it as one who knows that this life is not everything and that one day you will be again with those you have loved and lost awhile.

One pastor tells of a wife who lost her husband shortly after they celebrated their fiftieth wedding anniversary. For some time she lived in lonely retirement, but one day she came to the church with a new radiance on her face. When asked the reason for her happiness she said, "Why, Pastor, I have determined not to let three months of loneliness spoil the memories of fifty years of happiness." She had stored up memories to live by and was going to make the most of them through the days of separation.

A woman who had lost her son once asked, "Why did my boy die? Some people have told me that I loved him too much, that God wanted him; but I wanted him too. Others have said that I sinned and that is why I am being punished." A wise friend replied, "I can't tell you why it happened, but sorrow has come. How are you going to use it?" "Use it?" she asked. "Yes, use it. Sorrow has come to you, but it can make you face life with a larger heart and deeper sympathy and a greater understanding." She gripped his hand and went out and eventually did learn to use her sorrow and to be a blessing to others in their hours of grief.

Cherish your memories, thank God for them, and feel free to talk with others about the one you have loved and lost. Do not bottle it all up inside yourself. Express the thoughts of your heart and your mind and the one you have lost will become all the dearer as the days go by. As you accept the fact of death and take the strength and help that God can give, you will learn for yourself that the one you have lost seems close and strangely dear. Though you have lost the physical presence, the one who has gone ahead will seem close in spirit, and that comradeship will grow more blessed as the days go by. Live in the spirit of the one who said:

> Should you go first and I remain
> To walk the road alone,
> I'll live in memory's garden, dear,
> With happy days we've known.
> In Spring I'll wait for roses red
> When fades the lilac's blue,
> In early Fall when brown leaves call
> I'll catch a glimpse of you.

Should you go first and I remain
For battles to be fought,
Each thing you've touched along the way
Will be a hallowed spot.
I'll hear your voice, I'll see your smile,
Though blindly I may grope,
The memory of your helping hand
Will buoy me on with hope.

Should you go first and I remain
To finish with the scroll,
No length'ning shadows shall creep in
To make this life seem droll.
We've known so much of happiness,
We've had our cup of joy,
And memory is one gift of God
That death cannot destroy.

Should you go first and I remain,
One thing I'd have you do;
Walk slowly down the path of death,
For soon I'll follow you.
I'll want to know each step you take
That I may walk the same,
For some day down that lonely road
You'll hear me call your name.

Death will come. It comes to some who are young, some who are old. If you are young and have children when you lose your mate, keep the family together if you possibly can. Some of our finest and most heroic characters are men and women who have lost their life partner and are facing as best they can the problem of keeping the family together. Sometimes to help to that end it is wise to marry again. If true love comes, there may be an opportunity for one who has not yet been married to share the joys of marriage and the responsibility of raising the children.

Marry again if you are sure you have found the right person, but do not do it too quickly lest you make a mistake. I think of one man who married too soon a woman who was superficially sympathetic and understanding but with whom he had almost nothing in common. He married for the sake of the children only to find that she did not like children. If he had only waited he would probably have found someone much more suitable and he and his children would have been far happier.

Sometimes the children need to be reminded that it is right for their father or mother to remarry. One man whose wife had died when his children were grown and married and in homes of their own finally decided to marry again. The children objected vigorously. They did not like her and they felt it violated the memory of their mother for him to marry someone else. Yet none of the children wanted the father in their own homes though he was facing a life of loneliness. Very wisely he listened to all they had to say and then announced quietly, "I expect to marry her. I hope you will understand and will learn to love her as I do." Through the years she proved to be a companion and helpmate both for him and for his children. Remarriage, of course, is not always wise but the younger generation should be sure before objecting that they are genuinely concerned for the elder's happiness.

If you do not remarry, for the rest of your years on earth fill your life with good things. Get back quickly into some place of service. Go back to your church, the sooner the better. Do not put it off for fear of some of the associations there, for they will be among the most blessed memories of your love and life together.

It may be that you will seek employment or find some new channel of usefulness in the church or community. Forget yourself in love and service. In the comradeship and fellowship of the church of Christ you will find many people who are walking the same road and know the same loneliness and hunger of heart. You will find a faith that will carry you on until one day the lonely years will end and you too will go "through the valley of the shadow of death" to the one you love.

In the play by Channing Pollock entitled *Shining Armor,* the reality of such a reunion is beautifully portrayed. The action of the play takes place on two levels of the stage. Archie, the husband, dies toward the end of the story and goes on to his eternal home. In the closing scene on the lower stage you see his wife, tired and weary, resting in the little home she and Archie had built together. As she rests darkness falls and you sense that she has gone. Soon the upper stage glows with a heavenly light. There stands Archie, his face wreathed in smiles and his arms outstretched. From the shadows steps the woman he loves. He reaches out his hand and takes hers, she links her arm in his in the old way they knew, and they go on down the road together into eternity.

"Now abideth faith and hope and love and the greatest of these is love," for love is eternal and it holds God's answer to the lonely years.

XII

The Golden Years

AN OLDER minister from a nearby city who was talking with me in my study one day suddenly looked at his watch, rose from his chair and said, "I must go now." I asked, "What's the hurry?" He explained with a smile, "You see, today is our wedding anniversary. On this day every year since our marriage I have come into the house quietly just before dinner and seated myself at the piano. As I play the wedding march my wife comes marching to my side with a smile on her face and the light of love in her eyes just as she did many years ago when first we were married. Once again we pledge life and love to each other and in prayer renew our wedding vows. I wouldn't miss it for anything." You can understand why I hurried him on his way to such a happy occasion. He and his wife were not just looking toward a golden wedding anniversary. They were enjoying the golden years of mature life and love. They had learned how to grow old and how to grow old together.

As I watched him go I thought again of the lasting wonder and beauty of Christian marriage and a Christian home. "The love of Jesus, what it is, only his loved ones know." What miracles he works in lives and in homes that are open to his coming! The spirit of Christ can help you to find the best of love and to build an enduring home. Such is the miracle of the Christian home for all who face the sunset years, the golden years of life together.

It is strange that while most people want to live a long time, many are loath to accept the fact that to live longer you must grow older. But from the very moment of your birth you start growing older, and there really is nothing you can do about it except to learn the right way to grow old. Since that is true, there are certain questions all married couples should face as they look ahead to the long years of life together. How can one grow old gracefully and gratefully? How do you grow lovely growing old? How can couples be sure they will grow together as they grow older? How can you be certain that you will love each other all the more when you begin to find "silver threads among the gold"?

How wonderful it would be if all lovers could say with Channing Pollock in *Shining Armor*:

> Oh, could I live my life again,
> A life complete—three score and ten,
> The gift I'd ask from Him above
> Is that I might but have your love.
>
> For with it I am brave to go
> Out in the world—meet any foe,
> Without it I am worse than lost,
> And dread to reckon up the cost.
>
> So pledge me now your love anew,
> As I pledge mine, so strong and true,
> And through the years that stretch ahead,
> I'll love you as the day we wed.

Many through the years have learned something of the secret of growing old gracefully from one who did it so well himself that for nineteen hundred years men and women have read his words to catch the secret of life that he had found. "Forgetting what lies behind and straining forward to what lies ahead I press on toward the goal for the prize of the upward call of God in Christ Jesus. Let those of us who are mature be thus minded" (Philippians 3:13, 14). The Apostle Paul lived up to that ideal so well that when he finally came to the end of his earthly journey he could say, "I have fought a good fight, I have finished my course, I have kept the faith. Henceforth there is laid up for me a crown of righteousness" (II Timothy 4:7). Paul had learned how to grow old the right way.

So had a lovely Christian woman who, as she grew older, realized that her friends were growing older too, but that many of them were facing life gallantly and beautifully. She wanted to live that way herself and expressed her resolve in this manner:

> There are so many souls that go
> Gallantly and gay to meet old age.
> So many that pin courage over woe
> And bravely wage their fight on fear,
> Bearing aloft each day their flight of song
> That, self, we must throughout the years
> Refuse to be less strong.
>
> So let us keep, like them, an open mind,
> A heart of laughter and a reverent soul;
> Never think ourselves too busy to be kind.
> Let us so play life's strange and final role
> That younger people watching us will say,
> We would not mind it, growing old that way.

How are you going to grow old? Will your children and your life partner be happy or sad as they watch you meet the challenge of the years? As Marie Dressler once said, "The real question is not, how old you are, but how you are old."

One thing you must do is to accept the fact that there is no fountain of perpetual youth. Even if there were, eternal youth would not be the way to happiness in life. The golden years can be filled with so many good things that you can say, "Grow old along with me, the best is yet to be," and believe it and mean it. So many older couples live lives of rare beauty. They are lovely, they are friendly, there is a serenity about them and a peace and strength and assurance that inspires others. They grow more generous, more kindly, more understanding as they grow older.

Sad to say, there are others whose lives dry up and narrow down. They grow more self-centered, more selfish. There is so much of bitterness in their spirit that no one wants to be with them. They are just problems in other people's lives, rather than answers to other people's problems. You choose which you are going to be, and the lives of others are blessed or blighted by your choice.

Life expectancy has increased tremendously in the last half century and the average couple can look forward to long years of life together. Because you live now instead of fifty years ago, you have a chance at twenty more years of life than your forefathers could expect. In the days of Rome, the average life expectancy was only thirty years, and anyone who lived to be fifty was an exception. Now your life expectancy, if you are a woman, is seventy-one. If you are a man, it is sixty-five, and there are thousands who live far beyond those years. Back in 1880, 3.6 per cent of the people of this country were sixty-five years or over, one in twenty-seven. In 1940, that percentage had risen to 6 per cent, one in seventeen. By 1960 it will have been 10 per cent and one person in ten will have reached sixty-five years of age or over.

Since medical science has so extended the span of life that most of us are going to live a long time, it behooves us to learn how to do it better as individuals and as couples. Karle Wilson Baker wrote these lines entitled "Let Me Grow Lovely":

> Let me grow lovely growing old.
> So many fine things do;
> Laces and ivory and gold and silks
> Need not be new.
> There is healing in old trees.
> Old streets a glamor hold.
> Why may not I as well as they
> Grow lovely growing old.[1]

You can do just that in your home if you learn certain basic lessons in living. The first is to accept the fact that you are growing older. No matter what your age may be, it is folly to rebel against this fact of life. Believe in yourself and no matter what your years may be you can still feel that God has a place of usefulness for you. What this can mean is demonstrated in the life of Dr. F. W. Boatwright who for sixty-eight years was connected with the University of Richmond, for fifty-one years as president, and who continued to serve the institution, even in retirement, until the very day of his death. To understand the secret of his long and useful life, one must go back to the day when as a boy he was walking along a fence on the side of a millrace and fell in. He was carried on down the stream for some distance and washed up on a sand bar. His

[1] Reprinted with permission of the author.

people thought he was dead and took him home, put him in a casket and announced his funeral. Fortunately, he had not drowned, but had just been stunned. In the night he awoke and cried out. His father came and picked him up out of the coffin, amazed but grateful he was still alive. Dr. Boatwright, in telling of the incident, would say with a smile, "God must have spared me for something." That sense of destiny helped him to maintain his balance and his understanding, to grow in tolerance and in wisdom, in patience and in self-discipline all through the years of his notable career as a leader in Christian education.

You and I may not be spared as miraculously as that, but each Christian should feel a similar sense of divine destiny. As a child of God you rightly feel that He has made you for a place of worth and usefulness in life and no matter what your age may be, you feel that you are precious in His sight.

It is also important as you grow older to maintain the zest for living, to keep your sense of humor, to know that you can still find joy in life even though your activities may change, your physical vitality may lessen, and you have to rest a little more and relax a little longer. You can enjoy life no matter what your years may be, and your life partner, your children, and your grandchildren can all rejoice that you have been spared to them through the years.

An older minister's wife who is doing just that and doing it beautifully, said recently, "Well, you know I'm old, but I'm enjoying being old." Then with a smile on her face she gave this rhyme about herself:

> Nobody knows and nobody cares what an old woman wears,
> So I just go around and do as I please
> With my hair yanked back and my mind at ease.
> But now and then the old spirit burns,

And for velvets and laces my fancy turns.
So with earrings bobbing and my hair all curled,
I go out and smile on the great, big world.
But nobody knows and nobody cares—
An old woman's old no matter what she wears.

She laughed as she said it, for she has kept her zest for living and her children and her grandchildren and a host of friends are blessed by her spirit.

It is also important to keep your mind alert and growing. "Old age is not nearly as much a matter of hardening of the arteries as it is the hardening of ideas." Keep your mind alert and keep learning. As a couple, continue to seek new things to do and discuss together. As a matter of fact, you can learn many things much better when you are older if you just keep your mind open and working. The older you get the more things you can have to do and think about.

One of the best guarantees of happiness and respect in old age is to make memory your servant and not your master. Do not make the mistake of always living in the past and saying, "Well, now, this is the way we did it when I was a boy." Live for the future as well as for the past, making memory serve you, and patiently and humbly teach the lessons of the past to those who are facing the problems of today. One of the signs of maturity in youth is being willing to listen and to profit from the experience of others without having to go through some of the same harrowing events personally.

Be sure to act your age. Be yourself and proud of it. It is foolish to pretend you are younger. Be proud of the lines that nature carves in your features. You might as well, because those lines are going to come anyway.

As you grow older be a part of something greater than

yourself. Many today are retired from business when they still have much to give, and there are others whose family duties have lessened. Through the church and other agencies in the community they find many places open to those who want to continue active and useful in life. Just to prove what age can do, think of Michelangelo. Our family once climbed up inside the dome of the great cathedral he built in Florence, Italy. To give added strength he really constructed two domes, one inside the other; and visitors climb up between the two for a magnificent view from the top. When Michelangelo had finished that task he thought it was his crowning masterpiece, but he went on at eighty years of age to build St. Peter's in Rome.

Yes, there are wonderful things that age can do. You may not build a great cathedral, but you can build yourself into the lives of your children and of others who need you and find increasing joy through the years and new ways of growing and serving. Ethel R. Peyser made this her prayer when she wrote "When I Grow Old":

> When I grow old,
> God grant that every child
> Will feel the youthful texture of my soul
> And will not turn from me
> As from a shade or shrunken vine.
> When I grow old,
> God grant that I may have
> Some task which must be done
> Or someone fare the worse;
> That in some corner of the earth
> Someone will need my hand
> When I grow old.

While the two of you are growing older, be sure that you grow together. Mature love can be even finer and sweeter than youthful, romantic love. It can grow in depth and in understanding. When you are young your lives touch at a few very important points, but as you grow older life touches at every point. You share more of life together, your thoughts are blended in a deeper harmony and understanding, and life takes on a rare and rich beauty. Some couples not only come to think alike and feel alike, but they even begin to look alike because they really have become one. Such a love retains much of the beauty and all of the best of early romantic love. Its passion and its extravagant claims and promises may fade, but there is a growing respect and understanding, increasing tenderness and sympathy, and a true oneness in thinking, feeling, and acting.

Sad to say, too often that is not true. The mother gets so involved in the children and the cares in the home that she misses her chance for a growing comradeship with the man she loves. The husband gets so busy with business and outside interests that he grows away from the wife and family. Often the husband senses a declining vitality in life and begins to look elsewhere for physical satisfaction. The wife may go here, there, and everywhere trying to demonstrate to herself her own importance, or she languishes in a feeling of self-pity and inferiority because her children have grown and gone, she has no other interest in life, and she feels that no one wants her any more.

Love often withers and dies when the two are not consciously striving to grow and grow together. Love-making and love-breaking are very much akin. The same values enter in, but they are expressed in opposite ways. Love-making calls for kindness and consideration, unselfishness and tenderness, respect and devotion; but just the opposite of these will break love and ruin any relationship. Those who go through life "loyal and loving one to another" learn that that is the right way to grow together while growing old.

Many are the joys the passing years can bring to a Christian couple. What father would want to miss the thrill of pride and joy that is his as he walks down the aisle to give his daughter in marriage to the man she loves, or of serving as best man for his son on his wedding day?

What mother would want to miss the moving moment when she walks down the aisle on an usher's arm, perhaps her own son, and takes her place at the front to see her daughter come past the end of her pew and stand at the marriage altar as another Christian home is begun? In such an hour the cares of the years are forgotten in the joy that is yours and theirs.

Anniversaries, too, can be more than milestones of the passing years. They can be occasions for the reawakening of old memories and the renewing of the ties that bind your hearts in Christian love. One couple since their wedding day have observed not only the yearly anniversaries and such special occasions as the wooden, tin, and silver years, but also the day of the month on which they were married. Each month when that day comes he remembers her in some special way, a little gift, a dinner out, a treat for the family, or some simple token of his abiding and growing love. In leap years it is her turn. Thus they are journeying together through the golden years to the golden anniversary loving and loyal in spirit and in deed. The passing years in such a relationship are not deplored, but enjoyed by the two and the family as well.

As you grow together you will find that the golden years are increasingly filled with priceless memories as well as with new and happy experiences. As your children achieve independence and establish homes of their own you will have time and opportunity not only to enjoy their children with them but also to do together many of the things of which you have dreamed but that had to be postponed because of family responsibilities. Travel, community service, reading, hobbies, and creative opportunities will then be possible and will add to the joy and satisfaction of your life together. Many a church and community are blessed by those who have seized the golden opportunities the golden years afford to those who are willing to lose themselves in service for others only to find added joys for themselves in a feeling of continuing usefulness in life.

Truly there is no place like a Christian home. You, too, can make your marriage succeed in bringing joy and happiness to you, to those you love, and to countless others through the years. "Let this mind be in you which was also in Christ Jesus." Take as the rule of your life the words of Mary the mother of Jesus at the wedding in Cana of Galilee long ago, "Do what He tells you."

Those who build their marriage on the sure foundation of His truth and who live by His spirit will find the joys of love and home that only He can give and will have eternal and abiding joys the world can neither give nor take away. For them the golden years are a joy to themselves, an inspiration to others, and a foretaste of the joys and glories as yet unrevealed in the house not made with hands eternal in the heavens. Such is the spirit and promise of the hymn sung at many a wedding, "O Happy Home," by Karl J. Spitta:

O happy home, where Thou art loved the dearest,
Thou loving Friend and Saviour of the race,
And where among the guests there never cometh
One who can hold such high and honored place.

O happy home, where two in heart united,
In holy faith and blessed hope are one,
Whom death a little while alone divideth,
And cannot end the union here begun.

O happy home, where thou art not forgotten,
When joy is overflowing, full and free;
O happy home, where every wounded spirit
Is brought, Physician, Comforter, to Thee.

Until at last when earth's day's work is ended,
All meet Thee in the blessed home above.
From whence Thou camest, where Thou hast ascended,
Thy everlasting home of peace and love.

What such a faith can mean is seen in *Youth and the Homes of Tomorrow* as Dr. E. T. Dahlberg tells of the golden wedding anniversary of his parents. All the children and grandchildren came for the celebration. As all the family gathered for a last quiet vesper service, the mother prayed, "Dear Heavenly Father, we thank Thee that we have been permitted to live for Thee during these many years. Especially do we thank Thee for these days we have had together. Now, as we must part, grant that we may all meet again in the world to come and not one of us be absent."

With God's help and such a faith you can make your marriage succeed and increasing joys in life and love can be yours all the way from the thrilling days of falling in love to the crowning joys of the golden years. The secret of it all is summed up in these beautiful words from the Protestant Episcopal Marriage Commission:

> Christ at the marriage altar.
> Christ on the bridal journey.
> Christ when the new home is set up.
> Christ when the baby comes.
> Christ when the baby dies.
> Christ in the pinching times.
> Christ in the days of plenty.
> Christ when the wedded pair walk toward the sunset gates.
> Christ for time; Christ for eternity.
> This is the secret of home.

Some Helpful Books

FOR THE EARLY TEENS

Dickerson, R. E. *Growing into Manhood*. New York: Association Press.

From Boy to Man. Prepared by the American Social Hygiene Association, New York.

Klemer, Dora Hudson. *The Other Sex*. New York: Association Press.

Robinson, C. C. *A Boy and His Girl Friends*. New York: Association Press.

LOOKING TOWARD MARRIAGE

Adams, Clifford. *Preparing for Marriage*. New York: E. P. Dutton and Co.

Boone, W. C. *What God Hath Joined Together*. Nashville: Broadman Press.

Bowman, W. D. *Home Builders of Tomorrow*. Elgin, Ill.: Elgin Press.

Burkhart, Roy A. *From Friendship to Marriage*. New York: Harper & Brothers.

———. *The Secret of a Happy Marriage*. New York: Harper & Brothers.

———. *Thinking about Marriage*. New York: Association Press.

Dahlberg, E. T. *Youth and the Homes of Tomorrow*. Philadelphia: Judson Press.

Duvall, Evelyn Ruth, and Hill, R. L. *When You Marry*. Boston: D. C. Heath & Company.

Groves, E. R. *Preparation for Marriage*. New York: Emerson Books, Inc.

Popenoe, Paul Bowman. *Marriage Is What You Make It*. New York: The Macmillan Company.

SEX ADJUSTMENT

Butterfield, Oliver M. *Marriage and Sexual Harmony*. New York: Emerson Books, Inc.

Everett, M. S. *The Hygiene of Marriage*. Cleveland: World Publishing Company.

Lewin, S. A., and Gilmore, J. *Sex without Fear*. New York: Medical Research Press.

Popenoe, Paul Bowman. *Preparing for Marriage*. Institute of Family Relationships.

Stone, Hannah M. and Abraham. *A Marriage Manual*. New York: Simon & Schuster, Inc.

Van de Velde, T. H. *Ideal Marriage*. New York: Random House,

Wood, L. F., and Dickinson, R. L. *Harmony in Marriage*. New York: Round Table Press.

Wright, Helena B. *The Sex Factor in Marriage*. New York: Vanguard Press.

MARRIAGE AND THE HOME

Appelhof, Gilbert, Jr. *You Can Be Happily Married*. New York: The Macmillan Company.

Arden, T. Z. *Handbook for Husbands and Wives*. New York: Association Press.

Beaven, Albert W. *The Fine Art of Living Together*. New York: Harper & Brothers.

Himes, Norman E. *Your Marriage*. New York: Rinehart & Company.

Levy, John, and Munroe, Ruth. *The Happy Family*. New York: Alfred A. Knopf, Inc.

Overton, Grace Sloan. *The Home in a Changing Culture*. New York: Fleming H. Revell.

OF GENERAL INTEREST

Bowman, H. A. *Marriage for Moderns*. New York: McGraw-Hill.

Kling, Samuel G. and E. B. *The Marriage Guide*. New York: Prentice-Hall, Inc.

Popenoe, Paul Bowman. *Modern Marriage*. New York: The Macmillan Company.

Weatherhead, L. D., and Greaves, M. *The Mastery of Sex Through Psychology and Religion*. London: S. C. M. Press.

Set in Linotype Baskerville
Format by Marguerite Swanton
Manufactured by The Haddon Craftsmen, Inc.
Published by HARPER & BROTHERS, *New York*